EBURY PRESS

THE CLASS OF 83

S. Hussain Zaidi is India's number one crime writer. He is a veteran of investigative, crime and terror reporting. He is the author of several bestselling books, including *Dawood's Mentor*, *Dangerous Minds*, *Dongri to Dubai: Six Decades of the Mumbai Mafia*, *My Name Is Abu Salem* and *Black Friday*. He has worked for the *Asian Age*, *Mumbai Mirror*, *Mid-Day* and the *Indian Express*. He is also the associate producer for the HBO movie *Terror in Mumbai*, based on the 26/11 terror strikes. He lives with his family in Mumbai.

ALSO BY THE AUTHOR

Dawood's Mentor

Dangerous Minds

Dongri to Dubai: Six Decades of the Mumbai Mafia

My Name Is Abu Salem

Black Friday

S. HUSSAIN ZAIDI

THE CLASS OF 83

THE PUNISHERS OF MUMBAI POLICE

An imprint of Penguin Random House

EBURY PRESS

USA | Canada | UK | Ireland | Australia
New Zealand | India | South Africa | China

Ebury Press is part of the Penguin Random House group of companies
whose addresses can be found at global.penguinrandomhouse.com

Published by Penguin Random House India Pvt. Ltd
7th Floor, Infinity Tower C, DLF Cyber City,
Gurgaon 122 002, Haryana, India

First published in Ebury Press by Penguin Random House India 2019

10 9 8 7 6 5 4 3 2 1

This book is a work of non-fiction and is based on the evidence collected from a variety of sources, interviews conducted and personal interactions of the author with the various persons mentioned in the book. The views and opinions expressed in the chapters of this book are those of the author only and do not reflect or represent the views and opinions held by any other person.

This book is based on actual events and is based on evidence collected by the author with respect to the events enumerated. It reflects the author's representation of the events enumerated as truthfully as possible on the basis of the interviews conducted with various individuals and/or on the basis of materials that can be verified by research. All persons within the book are actual individuals.

The objective of this book is not to hurt any sentiments or be biased in favour of or against any particular person, society, gender, creed, nation or religion.

ISBN 9780143424277

Typeset in Adobe Garamond Pro by Manipal Technologies Limited, Manipal
Printed at Thomson Press India Ltd, New Delhi

www.penguin.co.in

To
Bilal Siddiqi, my protégé and friend,
who prevailed upon me to write this book.

Contents

1

IC 814 Hijack: The Mumbai Connection

On 24 December 1999, passengers onboard the Indian Airlines flight IC 814 from Kathmandu to Delhi were enjoying the mid-air meal service when five terrorists armed with guns and grenades pulled ski masks over their faces, rose from their seats and threatened the passengers and crew into submission. A bespectacled terrorist followed a crew member into the cockpit and pointed his weapon at the pilot. Seconds later, a sombre message was delivered over the public announcement system.

'Ladies and gentlemen, this is your captain. Our plane has been hijacked. Please be patient and listen to the hijackers.'

The hijackers ordered the pilot to continue flying west. Using the excuse of low fuel, the pilot diverted the flight to Amritsar where it could be refuelled. In reality, the pilot was trying to buy time for the Indian authorities to respond. When the plane was not refuelled after thirty minutes at Amritsar, the hijackers panicked that Indian special forces were preparing to storm the aircraft. They demanded that the plane take off from Indian soil immediately. To prove that they would kill all passengers if their demand was not complied with, the hijackers stabbed a knife into the chest of an Indian national onboard the aircraft. The pilot had no option but to take off without refuelling.

The ill-fated IC 814 then made its way to Lahore, where the Pakistani authorities wanted the plane off its territory at all cost. The flight briefly halted in Dubai before finally touching down at Kandahar, Afghanistan, which was under the control of the Taliban at the time. As soon as the plane landed, Taliban fighters took offensive positions around the aircraft. Thousands of miles away from Kandahar, tremors from the IC 814 hijack were felt in Mumbai.

The alarm clock on Pradeep Sharma's wristwatch beeped. He forced his eyes open and glanced at the time—5 a.m. He'd only slept a few hours since the hijack. The lack of rest and the herculean task had fatigued him. In fact, since the afternoon of 24 December, he had stayed put in the office of the Criminal Intelligence Unit (CIU) which was in the premises of the Andheri Police Station. Sharma threw the thin blanket away and splashed some water on his face. A constable knocked on the door and placed a steaming cup of tea on Sharma's desk, right next to a typewriter-sized box which was connected to headphones.

Wireless tapping or electronic surveillance was at a nascent stage in those days. It could be done through a huge briefcase-like box connected to several wires and chords running in and out of it. Sharma sipped the tea, and the warmth refreshed him. He placed the cushioned headphones over his ears. Then he waited. For the last two days, at around this time, he had been intercepting the communications of Abdul Latif with his contacts based in Delhi and Pakistan. Soon enough, Abdul

Latif's voice cracked through the headphone. He was speaking to his Pakistani handler this time.

'*Mubarakbad, janab* (Congratulations, sir),' Latif said. '*Project bas khatam ho raha hai* (The project is about to be completed).'

'*Bahot khoob* (Very good),' the handler said. '*Saare bande mehfooz toh hai na*? (Is everyone okay?)'

Sharma clenched his fist. As per the demands of the terrorists, the Indian government was unenviably considering the release of three dreaded militants, including Maulana Masood Azhar, in return for the safety of around 190 civilians onboard IC 814. The relatives of the passengers had, understandably, launched a sustained campaign to get their loved ones released. Seething, Sharma heard the early morning azaan in the background of the call. *'Allahu Akbar! Allahu Akbar!'*

The muezzin was giving the clarion call to the believers to assemble for morning prayers before the break of dawn. Sharma was finding it difficult to eavesdrop on the conversation because of the loud azaan. He did not understand, then, that a divine hand was giving him a vital clue towards solving the most important case of his life. Like the muezzin, even animals wake up and make calls in their own way. There was another distinct sound that caught Sharma's attention—the mooing of cows and buffaloes.

Suddenly, Sharma perked up. He knew now that Latif's hideout was in a predominantly Muslim locality with a masjid and a *tabela* in the vicinity. Despite his fatigue and body ache, Sharma wanted to do cartwheels in the air. The azaan was over, the conversation became clear again.

'*Yaad rahe* Abdul Latif,' the handler said, '*hamari manzil Kandahar ke bhi aage hai* (Remember Latif, our destination is beyond Kandahar).'

'*Insha Allah*,' Latif said and hung up.

Sharma placed the headphones back on the table. The Pakistan-backed terrorists had already pushed the Government of India into a corner in the hostile territory of Kandahar. And now they were planning something bigger. What was their mission? Surely, Latif's boastful voice signified something of great magnitude. What could garner more attention to the cause of the terrorists than the hijack of an Indian Airlines flight? The question itself was scary. And Sharma was desperate to find the answer.

A few days ago, immediately after the hijack, Pradeep Sharma had received a call from Hemant Karkare who had recently moved to the Research and Analysis Wing (RAW). Sharma had served under Karkare in the Anti-Narcotics Cell (ANC) of the Mumbai police crime branch and had immense respect for the senior officer. On the call, Karkare had asked Sharma to meet him at a pre-decided location in utmost secrecy. Sharma gauged the seriousness of the call by the fact that Karkare had especially flown down from Delhi to Mumbai. During the meeting, Karkare handed Sharma a slip of paper with a phone number written on it.

'This number belongs to one Abdul Latif,' Karkare said. 'The man has links to the Kandahar hijacking.'

'And Latif is in Mumbai?'

'Yes,' Karkare said. 'Find him.'

'Do we have a location?'

'He is in Mumbai,' Karkare said. 'I have nothing more.'

'A photograph? Description?'

Karkare shook his head. 'Zilch.'

Sharma understood the gravity of the problem. He was being asked to find a man in city with over 10 million people and all he had was a name and a phone number. These were times when Internet penetration in India was very low. Social media was virtually non-existent so Sharma couldn't have put a name into a search engine or a social network to see what popped up. But Sharma understood that the very complexity of the problem was why Karkare had reached out to him. Finding a man with only a phone number in hand required a certain resourcefulness that Karkare could have expected only out of Sharma.

Sharma did not know whether he should interpret it as a compliment or Karkare's desperation that he had only one man he could trust in this huge city with 38,000 policemen, including 5000 officers.

The RAW at the time did not have many local resources. So, the officers of the agency often reached out to local enforcement officers for assistance. In fact, Sharma knew that Hemant Karkare would go out of the way to support him if push came to shove. So, Sharma did not disappoint Karkare by asking for written orders, clearances and other permissions. He only stood up and saluted his senior.

'I will get you this man, sir,' Sharma said, even though he was not sure how he was going to do so.

'*Shabaash*,' Karkare said. 'Keep it confidential, Pradeep. This is a matter of national security.'

Initially, Sharma's search for Abdul Latif led him to many dead ends. The phone number turned out to be a prepaid number which had been issued without proper scrutiny of the address. These were early days for the mobile service providers in India. Document verification was not stringent. Sharma tapped his entire network of informants but gave them only the details they needed to know without revealing the context.

Sharma's hunch was that Latif was in a Muslim dominated locality near a mosque. The possibilities of this theory were endless. In fact, every Muslim dominated locality would have a mosque nearby, similar to other religions and their places of worship. Yet, Sharma made one of his most trusted informers, Saleem, speak with many imams of mosques in the suburbs to find out if any suspicious person had turned up to offer namaz at their mosque recently. Saleem also got in touch with several real estate agents to see if any untoward person had rented out a flat in their locality. But unfortunately, no leads emerged from these efforts.

In 1998, the Mumbai Police had come across a bizarre case of a bleeding man walking out of a toilet of a masjid in south Mumbai. It turned out that the man was trying to assemble explosives in the toilet, and it had detonated accidentally and injured him. The bleeding man abruptly left his device in the toilet and escaped on foot, while his white clothes were drenched with blood and he was bleeding all over his face and neck. Then Police Commissioner R.H. Mendonca and Crime Chief R.S. Sharma had stepped into a Mumbai masjid for the first time to inspect the spot. However, the crime branch eventually found out that it was a Pakistani who had been staying in a Muslim locality in Nirmal Nagar in Santacruz for six months with a different name.

Sharma presumed that people who visited mosques frequently would notice a stranger and they would share this information with the police. But this time Sharma drew a blank. The only fall-back option now was the mobile number Karkare had given him. Back then there weren't any sophisticated cell-phone tapping capabilities, but Sharma had managed to procure a crude telephone tapping equipment from his sources in the department and set it up in the CIU office at Andheri. Over a listening period of two days, Sharma had figured out that Latif was in an area which had a mosque nearby because the azaan of morning prayer could be heard distinctly in the background. The area also had a cowshed nearby because the mooing of cows and buffaloes was loud and clear. Sharma called a team of constables into his cabin.

'How many mosques in Mumbai have a cowshed nearby?' he asked.

His men were stunned by the question. They were unsure if Sharma was testing their knowledge as many Mumbaikars take immense pride in knowing trivial details about the city like the routes of the BEST buses, the famous delicacies of each area, renowned roadside shops located in the many bylanes of Mumbai. The constables merely smiled and stared back at Sharma.

'No one is allowed to go back home until I have this information,' Sharma said, looking serious.

The constables rushed out of his room. In a few hours, they reported back to Sharma. There were five possible areas matching his description: Cheetah Camp in Mankhurd, Kurla Pipe Road, Amrut Nagar in Mumbra, Thane, and places in Jogeshwari and Goregaon.

Sharma had been continually discussing the case with Hemant Karkare, who was aghast to hear that the terrorists had bigger plans up their sleeves. Kandahar was being tracked by media across the globe. Already, India was being portrayed as a soft state which had been forced to the negotiating table by a rogue group of terrorists. Prime Minister Atal Bihari Vajpayee had stepped down from his aggressive posturing that the Indian government would not engage in any negotiations under the threat of the gun. Now, the government was seeking solace in the fact that the terrorists had apparently scaled down many of their demands. India's image was being tarnished by the international media.

But the government was also concerned for the lives of the 190 civilians. The Indian national whom the hijackers had stabbed had bled to death. The innocent man was returning from his honeymoon trip with his newly wed wife. The pressure on the government was immense, and it was understandable that the lives of the citizens were being made a priority over other considerations. Indian agencies like RAW had also taken a severe beating that an incident like this had occurred in the first place. Meanwhile, Sharma briefed Karkare about the four locations he had zeroed in on. But launching a manhunt at these locations required sizeable manpower which could compromise the secrecy of Karkare's mission.

'We can't take any more damage,' Karkare told Sharma.

'Sir, I am close to catching our man.'

'Pradeep, only the result will count!' Karkare said. 'What is your next plan of action?'

'I'm tapping my resources in the telecom operator to get a tower location on Latif's number.'

'Time is against us,' Karkare replied. 'Arrest Latif at all costs and soon.'

The tower location was eventually found. Latif was making those early morning calls from the Behram Baug area near Jogeshwari west. Sharma prepared a list of Muslim dominated areas around this locality which had a mosque and a cowshed in the vicinity. Behram Baug was a densely populated locality with labyrinthine streets and *chawls*, making it difficult to pinpoint a particular house. Immediately, Sharma dispatched his informer

Saleem to dig up more information. This time, Sharma hit the jackpot. Saleem found out from a real estate agent that a couple of men had recently moved into a room in a chawl in Behram Baug, and 'something' was off about them. The room in question belonged to one Mushtaq Ahmed Azmi.

Based on Saleem's information, Sharma put the men in Behram Baug under surveillance. If Sharma made a wrong arrest, it would be all over the newspapers and the real terrorists would get wind that the police were on their tail. And time was running out. Sharma discussed the situation with Karkare once again.

'Go for the arrest,' Karkare said, crisply. 'But keep your guns under control.'

A team of Indian negotiators, which included then Intelligence Bureau (IB) Chief Ajit Doval, landed in Kandahar to resolve the hijacking crisis. The aircraft used by the negotiating team was also carrying National Security Guard (NSG) commandoes who were trained to handle hijacking situations. But the offensive positions taken by the Taliban fighters around IC 814 dithered the assault plans of the special forces. Though the Taliban maintained that they had surrounded the aircraft to prevent the hijackers from killing passengers, their role was suspected to be diabolical by the Indian authorities. Three militants, including Maulana Masood Azhar, were handed over to the hijackers to save the civilians onboard the flight. The five hijackers used a Taliban hostage to secure their passage out of Afghanistan. The passengers of IC 814 were brought back to India on 31 December 1999.

Abdul Latif was waiting for a local train at Jogeshwari station. The platform was full of daily commuters. The train whistled aloud as it chugged towards the station. The train hadn't even halted completely but adept Mumbaikars were already alighting and boarding the cramped compartments, jostling for space. Latif went straight into the mix, trying to secure a place on the footboard when a hand grabbed his shirt collar and pulled him back. This was not an abnormal sight on Mumbai's local railway station where getting into a train is no less than a daily verbal battle and an occasional fistfight.

But much to Latif's horror, it wasn't a co-passenger who had stopped him from boarding the train. Latif turned around and found himself staring into Pradeep Sharma's snarling face.

Sharma tightened his grip on Latif's collar. He dragged Latif along the platform and a police team surrounded the terrorist from all sides. Commuters hanging out of the compartments watched horrified as the train pulled away from Jogeshwari station. Latif realized that his game was over. He put up no resistance and was quickly bundled into a waiting police vehicle.

During his interrogation, Latif revealed that he had indeed been involved with the Kandahar conspiracy. He was working for the Inter-Services Intelligence (ISI) and had worked out the logistics of the hijacking. The men who were staying with him in Behram Baug were also ISI operatives.

More shocking details emerged. A couple of months ago, four armed men had looted 7.52 lakh rupees from a cooperative bank in Borivali. The money was then used to fund the hijacking of IC 814. The robbers had also snatched an employee's identity, which was used to procure the SIM card with which Latif was making the local calls. He also obtained licences in the hijackers' name from a driving school in Jogeshwari. The licenses were then used to arrange passports for the hijackers. A posse of weapons and explosives was stored in the room at the chawl in Behram Baug. Pradeep Sharma was stunned. He had to act fast.

A heavily armed police team led by Sharma stealthily descended upon Latif's hideout in Behram Baug. Sharma made his way into the narrow chawl, followed by his men, and half squatted near the window of the room where the ISI agents were holed up. Then, he peered inside. He could not believe the sight.

A man wearing a kurta pyjama was callously tossing a grenade in the air and catching it. The man had no fear that the grenade could possibly burst and kill everyone around him. Sharma's belief that they were fighting an enemy who had no fear of death was reinforced. There was another man in the room, and Sharma could see the skin on his soles had dried and chipped away as result of exposure to severe cold. This man had the sinewy build and the fair face of mountain folk. He could possibly be a *mujahideen* fighter from the snowy regions of Kashmir or even Afghanistan.

Sharma turned around to look at his men. They were waiting for his command. He gripped his weapon, not knowing what would happen once they walked through the door. On his signal, the police team burst into the room with their guns drawn. Sharma was anticipating a gunfight but the men in the room were caught unaware. They raised their hands in the air and gave up without a fight!

On searching the room, Sharma and his team found the photographs of the IC 814 hijackers. The room was also stocked with AK-56 rifles, hand grenades and other ammunition. Sharma was surprised that such well-armed enemies had not fired these weapons when the police had barged inside. One of the men arrested was identified as Rafiq Mohammed. Abdul Latif and Rafiq Mohammed were shown to be arrested on 30 December 1999.

Sharma then fitted in the final piece of the jigsaw. What was Latif's bigger plan? Further interrogation revealed that the ISI agents were planning an attack on Prime Minister Atal Bihari Vajpayee! The prime minister was due to visit Mumbai soon and an attack on his convoy had been planned. On the upcoming Republic Day, the ISI agents were also planning explosions in Mumbai and other cities, much like the Black Friday bomb blasts which happened in March 1993. Sharma heaved a huge sigh of relief that a major attack on the prime minister, and his own city of Mumbai, had been averted.

Hemant Karkare congratulated Sharma on busting an ISI module and failing their nefarious designs. Sharma was only thankful that he had lived up to the faith that Karkare had reposed in him. The photographs of the IC 814 hijackers were eventually passed onto L.K. Advani, the then deputy prime minister of India and the home minister in the central government. The pictures were used by India in the United Nations (UN) to build a case against the cross-border support that the hijackers had received.

Then Home Minister of Maharashtra, Chhagan Bhujbal, drove all the way from Mantralaya to Andheri and examined the rifles, grenades, detonators and explosives that had been recovered from Behram Baug. Bhujbal was thoroughly impressed by the Mumbai Police's work. Pradeep Sharma received a special pat on the back from the home minister of Maharashtra. At a huge press conference, Bhujbal also announced a cash reward of Rs 5 lakh for Sharma.

Till date, Pradeep Sharma has not received the cash reward but he is satisfied that he contributed significantly in preventing a terrorist attack on the sovereignty of the nation and that he received appreciation from not only his seniors but also from the state's home minister. Sharma was glad that Hemant Karkare, with whom he shared excellent rapport, was soon posted as deputy director of RAW in Vienna, Austria. Sharma also appreciates that, true to the spirit of the nation, his Muslim informers played a vital role in cracking, perhaps, the biggest case of his life.

Unlike other famous and elite cops of Mumbai, Sharma was a rank outsider.

A rare success story, Sharma would have been a Chemistry professor in some rural college but for his rebellious and iconoclastic instincts. It all started on a dull day over a dozen years ago in the nondescript suburbs of Mumbai.

2

First Blood

A multitude of tiny, colourful bulbs glittered above the central dome of the Pankhe Shah Dargah at Vikhroli. In 1990, the sixtieth annual *urs* (wedding ritual) of Saint Syed Tajammul Hussain, popularly known as Pankhe Shah Baba (the seer of fans) was at its peak. Not much is known as to why the seer was revered with such a name except that he was seen with a hand-held fan trying to comfort himself. But on this day, a lesser known mortal was going to win lot of followers—or fans—at the door of the saint's tomb.

A beautiful *qawwali* rang through the crowded lanes. Two singers sang atop a red pandal hoisted outside the dargah. Hordes of listeners revelled in the music, thoroughly mesmerized. The supporting musicians fanned their harmoniums. The most supplicatory qawwali of the Indian subcontinent enthralled the Muslim devotees.

Bhar do jholi meri ya Mohammad,
Laut kar mai na jaaoonga khali

(Fulfil my request, O Prophet Mohammad,
For I will not return empty handed.)

Many years ago, this qawwali was used in a popular Bollywood movie; the lyrics written originally by Purnam Allahabadi were made famous by the voice of the Sabri Brothers from Pakistan. The rendition of this song at the Pankhe Shah Dargah reached a crescendo, drawing praise and admiration from the devotees who had come for *ziyarat* (pilgrimage). Outside the shrine, a fleet of shops sold *halwa paratha*, *petha* and other savouries. A makeshift photo studio flaunted life-size cut-outs of reigning superstars Amitabh Bachchan and Hema Malini. Visitors lined up for a photograph with their matinee idols. But this festive atmosphere was going to change in the next few moments.

At Ghatkopar Police Station, Sub Inspector (SI) Pradeep Sharma slumped into the chair behind his desk. The past three months at the police station had been uneventful. He was merely killing time, waiting for his shift to end so that he could go home. He spun a paperweight on its axis. The heavy object turned like a top on the wooden table before rattling to a stop. Seven years since donning the khaki uniform, this postgraduate in MSc had only served on routine night patrols and *bandobust* duties. He was about to leave for the day when the telephone on his desk rang aloud. Sharma picked up the handset and held it against his ear. He recognized the voice that greeted him. It was one of his most trusted informants.

'Sir,' the informant said, 'those two men who are the talk of the town these days?'

'Javed and Raju?' Sharma said. 'Are you sure?'

'Yes, they are evicting people in chawls opposite Pankhe Shah Dargah,' said the informant. 'Hundred and ten percent, sir.'

Sharma slammed the handset back into the cradle. He ran his thumb and forefinger over his bushy moustache. Arresting these two wanted criminals would be his first major catch. He sprang from his chair, shouting orders at three constables who were standing in the corridor and talking among themselves. Sharma's thunderous voice moved the constables into action. Sharma did not want to be like the police team usually portrayed in the movies; always reaching much later, invariably after the oppressors had decamped.

Within minutes, Sharma and his three constables were huddled into the police jeep and speeding towards Pankhe Shah Dargah.

As the qawwali concluded, people started to leave through the shrine's narrow corridor which led towards the main highway, Agra Road. Considered India's longest highway, it connected to the city of the Taj Mahal which was 1300 kilometres away from Mumbai. It was yet to be renamed LBS Marg. The crowd gathered on the main road. Some walked towards the Sanghani bus stop, while others strolled to the nearby Ghatkopar station on foot. Still others walked towards their vehicles or bicycles. A few rummaged their pockets for cigarettes, *bidi*s and other oral vices. Precisely at this moment, people witnessed a bedlam across the dargah. No one dared to intervene. Most men turned their backs and walked away. But who could blame them? Not many men had the fortitude to stand up to Javed Khan and his friend, Raju.

The burly Javed rested his back against the hood of a black and yellow taxi. A wicked smile played on his lips. He brandished a revolver in his right hand, which was resting at a comfortable angle, and enjoyed the spectacle in front of him. A few metres away, Raju came out of a house with a stack of clothes in his hands. His merciless laughter echoed through the air. An old woman followed him, her hands folded. Helpless cries streamed from her wrinkled lips. Raju dumped the clothes on the ground and went back inside the house, roughly brushing past an old man who trembled out of sheer terror. The old couple's house had fallen into the sights of a corrupt builder. The builder had hired Javed and Raju to evict the couple from their premises.

Javed and Raju, both in their thirties, were among the most feared names in the Mumbai underworld. Their unspeakable atrocities included raping a woman in front of her husband and then slitting his throat in front of her. They had scant regard for human life. No fear of the authorities. They were mercenaries for gangs who needed guns for hire, or for rich men who needed muscle for dirty jobs.

Only a few months ago, Javed had escaped from Aurangabad's Harsul Central Jail while Raju, a known history sheeter, was also wanted in several cases. Since Raju was a common name, he was identified by the alias *Najma ka Raju* (Najma's son Raju) after his mother. The police in Mumbai, Thane as well as Aurangabad had received inputs indicating that the duo had fled to Mumbai. Hence, every cop in Mumbai was instructed to look out for them, along with the caveat—be careful, they are always heavily armed. The gun in Javed's hand, as well as the sword that Raju was carrying, was a testament to this.

One after another, Raju threw the old couple's belongings out of the house. The old man fell at the gangster's feet and begged for mercy. Raju lifted his foot and kicked the old man in his face. The man rolled to a distance, his hand on his nose to stem the flow of blood. The old woman grabbed her husband to prevent him from further harm. Raju began throwing the kitchen utensils on the road. The old couple were left with no option except to bow to the gangsters' demands. Javed and Raju dragged the old man and woman along the road, intending to bundle them into the waiting taxi with a one-way ticket to nowhere. The entire locality stood and watched the atrocities that Javed Khan and Raju had unleashed against a feeble couple.

Crossing the busy intersection of Sarvodaya Hospital, the siren blaring police jeep reached the lanes leading up to Pankhe Shah Dargah. Sharma sensed a commotion ahead. The van screeched to a halt only metres away from where Javed and Raju were forcing the old couple inside the taxi. The two gangsters turned around and snarled at the sight of the policemen. Cursing, they pushed the old couple away and ran towards the van.

In those days, an attack on the cops was totally unimaginable. In fact, no criminal in his right mind would even think of glaring at an angry policeman. Mumbai Police had already encountered a few wanted criminals. Manya Surve at Wadala and Rama Naik at Chembur were recent cases of police action. Word had spread among the underworld that if they went too far, the police would encounter them. These encounters had instilled a sense of fear in the criminals' minds, which, in turn, gave the police a newfound feeling of power.

Thus, Sharma's team was not expecting the two criminals to launch an all-out offensive. The police party jumped out of the van, ordering Javed and Raju to surrender. But the gangsters were high on the might of their weapons. They responded only with the choicest of expletives. The first constable charged towards Raju, who raised his sword high above his head and swung it in an arc. The sharp blade whipped through the air and cut across the constable's arm. A fountain of blood erupted. The constable fell and began dragging himself back towards the safety of the police van. Raju followed the constable with a menacing smile across his blood-smeared face. The second constable rushed to help his fallen colleague. Raju slashed his sword again. And the second constable's uniform was drenched in his own blood.

The third constable found himself staring into the cruel mask of Raju's face. He turned around to run away but the burly Javed had already blocked the constable's path. Javed aimed his gun at the constable. The shivering constable fell to his knees and started praying to his family deity. All of this had happened in a matter of seconds.

Paces away, Pradeep Sharma exited the jeep. He pulled out his service revolver from the holster on his hip. Easing into his shooting stance, he spread his legs shoulder-width. Now, he was standing square to Javed's position. His training took over his instincts, and his right foot moved slightly behind his left, supporting foot. His balance was immaculate. Inside his polished, brown shoes his toes were firm. He moved swiftly to get a better shot at his targets. His knees flexed as he inched closer to the spot. Leaning forward, he raised his weapon. The barrel of his gun was steady. His finger curled around the trigger. Before Javed could shoot the constable, Sharma fired thrice.

Two bullets tore through the bulk of Javed's body. One bullet created a small hole in his shoulder and exited from the back of his trapeze, the other one was embedded in his chest. Yet, the huge gangster stood on his feet for a few moments, rocking back and forth. Then he fell to the ground. Puffs of dust rose through the air.

Children started crying. Their mothers held them to their bosoms and rushed behind the cover of pillars and trees.

Damodar Park, the recently constructed high-rise behind the dargah, had a clear view of the scene. People peered out of their balconies and windows to see the police in action.

While on the road, Raju, for a moment couldn't believe what he had just seen. His friend's lifeless body was staring blankly at the sky.

The hot-blooded Raju threw all caution to the wind. He raised his sword with both hands and rushed towards Sharma, expletives streaming out his mouth. The gleam of Raju's sword blinded Sharma for a moment. But he was quick to adjust his position, keeping his head level. He fired two bullets again. Raju stopped in his tracks. Blood oozed out of his body. His sword clanged to the ground. He felt his torso with his hands, and looked at his palms which had now turned red. His knees wilted. He thudded to the ground, inches away from his fallen sword.

Finally, the third constable opened his eyes. Javed and Raju were lying on either side of him. Pools of blood formed under their bodies. He looked from one man to another, and then turned his gaze up. SI Pradeep Sharma was standing tall over the dead bodies of the two gangsters, his empty revolver still raised, the last wisp of smoke snaking out of the barrel and disappearing into the air.

The serious injury to two constables and a near death situation for his third man was enough to make Sharma's blood boil. Later in an interview, he admitted that he never intended to kill the two desperadoes. 'But I was left with no alternative but to open fire,' Sharma explained.

The killing of two Muslim criminals on the busy main road in front of a dargah could have become a communal flashpoint. But the whole locality erupted in joy and celebration. The old couple who were nearly evicted out of their house fell at

Sharma's feet. For them, he was an angel. One man picked up a garland from the dargah and placed it around Sharma's neck. The three injured cops forgot their suffering but were stupefied in awe of their officer's gumption. They began making arrangements for an ambulance to rush Javed and Raju to Rajawadi Hospital in Ghatkopar east for the treatment of their bleeding wounds.

Before getting back into his jeep, Sharma looked at the sky to express his gratitude to God. He had saved the life of the men he commanded, and perhaps the lives of many more innocents who could have become victims of these heartless gangsters. A young boy turned on the loudspeaker on the red pandal. The sound of the famous qawwali, once again, resonated through the air. In reverence, Sharma touched his forefinger to his chest and then his forehead.

Bhar do jholi meri Sarkare Madina,
Laut kar mai na jaaoonga khali…

(Fulfil my wishes, O Lord Medina,
as I will not return empty-handed…)

The jeep took off, leaving behind a plume of smoke.

3

Cage for a Cop

7 January 2010

Pradeep Sharma drank the last drops of tea from a porcelain cup at the office of K.M. Prasanna, Deputy Commissioner of Police (DCP). The beverage's unusually strong aftertaste settled on his tongue. He coughed. A stony silence had paused the ongoing conversation between the two police officers. Sharma placed the teacup back on the table.

Prasanna, the zonal in-charge, looked at Sharma with finality and said ominously, 'We will have to arrest you.'

Sharma leaned back in the chair and exhaled. His temple throbbed terribly. He had been mentally preparing for this announcement but hearing it was far worse than he had imagined. The uncomfortable hum of an old air conditioner in the office grew louder. Earlier in the day, he was called in for questioning. As a police officer, he was aware there was no compulsion for his arrest. He was not going to flee from the law or abscond from the country. But Sharma knew his fate had already been sealed, even if temporarily, by the senior officers of his department and the political authorities of the state.

Less than a month ago, on 24 December, *DNA*, a daily newspaper, now defunct, had published an article[1] about Mumbai Police personnel, including an Assistant Commissioner of Police (ACP), attending a Christmas party thrown by Paulson Joseph in Chembur where they were seen dancing and rubbing shoulders with known underworld figures. The article was accompanied by a grab from a video, which was shot at the party and had captured the cops' revelries.

The story was a huge slap in the face for the entire police force and interpreted as a huge blemish on the police top brass' reputation.

Sharma had read the news report with idle amusement. Being Sharma, he had also received the video on his phone by the end of the day. Those were the days before WhatsApp and this process had involved a chain of multiple people through which the video was passed on to his phone via Bluetooth.

He had known that the development would shake the police echelons and soon everyone would start looking for a scapegoat. The news media, and the government, bayed for blood. An inquiry was set up while the police went into damage control mode.

What Sharma was not prepared for was the fallout that bore directly on him. For some reason, certain sections of the Mumbai IPS lobby started suspecting that it was Sharma who had sent the video to *DNA*. Sharma had nothing to do with

[1] Nikhil S. Dixit, '"Aye" ACP, "chal Daru La"', *DNA* India, 26 December 2009 https://www.dnaindia.com/mumbai/report-aye-acp-chal-daru-la-1327899 (accessed 9 June 2019).

it and found the idea laughable. However, there were police officers who felt that Sharma was trying to engineer a shake up in the police hierarchy so that he could install his favourite boss, Satyapal Singh, at the helm. It was decided that Sharma needed to be gone, and fast.

And so, barely thirteen days later, Sharma was placed under arrest.

He held his composure and nodded in resignation. 'Alright, sir.'

After serving the Mumbai Police for twenty-six years and wreaking annihilation on various gangs in the city, killing over 111 gangsters and arresting over 1111 underworld operatives, Pradeep Sharma was arrested on the charges of killing a man in a fake encounter whom he had never seen in his life. The creases on Sharma's broad forehead furrowed. He had taken utmost pride in wearing the uniform. After serving the law all his life, he did not want his sterling career to culminate in him ending up as a criminal.

Half a dozen officers from Bandra Police Station at Hill Road, which was just below the office of the zonal DCP, entered the room. They surrounded Sharma from all sides. These were men whom he had served with, his brothers-in-arms. For a brief second, Sharma looked at each one of them, matching their gaze with his own. Some officers turned their eyes away, but a few other faces bore nothing but hostility for him.

Sharma was aware why so many men had surrounded him. This was an age-old strategy employed by cops against a criminal who they feared could become aggressive. Hence, in order to contain his aggression, this pre-emptive measure had been employed to intimidate Sharma and if need be, subdue him with use of necessary force. These men were under orders and would not hesitate to carry out their duties. All this Sharma understood perfectly. He was an officer of the law himself and knew that the chain of command had to be obeyed.

And then Sharma had an epiphany. Perhaps the powers that be felt that Sharma, known for his violent skirmishes with gangsters, would not give up so easily, and that he may attempt to escape from custody or shoot his way to freedom and flee. At that moment, a strangling sadness and a certain happiness flooded through his chest. Sadness because his department had totally disregarded the loyalty with which he had served for more than two and a half decades. Happiness because they had not taken him for granted, after all. But still the man of 111 encounters felt like a hail of bullets had been treacherously shot into his back. Perhaps this dishonour was worse than death.

Even in that traumatic moment, Sharma smiled to himself. He maintained his calm and anticipated that much worse was coming ahead. He braced himself for more humiliation. But his presence of mind had not deserted him even in such a tense situation. Sharma quietly put his hand under the table and began scrolling through his phone's picture gallery.

Unknown and unseen to Prasanna, Sharma was trying to delete a sensational picture from his phone gallery in which a MP from Mumbai was posing with Bunty Pandey, a member of the Chhota Rajan gang. Sharma knew that his phone would be seized after his arrest and it could be used as evidence. Discovery of such a scandalous photograph could be misinterpreted in myriad ways, including the presumption that he was collecting such material to blackmail powerful people.

Once Sharma deleted the picture from his phone, he requested the DCP to allow him to make a call to his wife, Swikriti, who had stood by him through thick and thin for over twenty years. The DCP granted his request. Sharma called his wife and briefly told her about his arrest. Then he told her something which stunned everyone, including the DCP, the police officers present in the room, as well as his wife.

'If you ever try to visit me either in court or in jail,' he said, 'I will shoot myself dead.'

Then, Sharma disconnected the phone. The calmness with which he had spoken the last line had made the officers look at each other with apparent curiosity. They wondered why a man like Sharma, who had decimated more than a hundred gangsters to survive, could talk about taking his own life so casually over such a trivial matter as his wife visiting him in court or jail? They weren't aware that Sharma wanted to fight this battle alone, just like he had fought so many others. He would brave the storm himself and did not want to burden his family under the avalanche of embarrassment and insults which were due to follow soon.

News of Sharma's arrest spread like wildfire. Soon, several television vans were parked outside the police station. Scores of reporters made a beeline for Senior Police Inspector (PI) Prakash George's cabin. A massive crowd of curious onlookers also thronged the police station. No one outside the premises knew why the number of people had begun to swell. A curious man in the crowd approached the constable manning the gates of the police station. 'Is Salman Khan being arrested again?' he asked.

The constable ignored the man and shut the entry to the police station to prevent the crowd outside from spilling into the compound. Only those who had genuine business were let inside.

Clarity prevailed only after many hours. Sharma had been arrested for the fake encounter of Ram Narayan Gupta alias Lakhan Bhaiyya, an alleged aide of Chhota Rajan, who was killed by officers and men of D.N. Nagar Police Station in 2006. Some thirteen cops were accused of the fake encounter, including Senior PI Pradeep Suryavanshi.

The most shocking aspect of Sharma's arrest was that none of the D.N. Nagar cops were detained or questioned intensively. Sharma became the first casualty in the case, and he was promptly arrested ahead of any others. Even by the principles of respondeat superior (where the leader is answerable for the team), the first man to be arrested should have been Senior PI Suryavanshi and not Sharma.

And Sharma was convinced that his arrest had nothing to do with the Lakhan Bhaiya encounter. However, Sharma's arrest seemed to be part of a much larger conspiracy than his involvement in a six-year-old encounter case. It did not require a brilliant analyst to figure out that Sharma was facing retribution for an entirely different case. The man was involved in over a hundred encounters. He had not landed in the dock in any of these cases, leave alone inquiry or departmental action.

The Mumbai media was totally familiar with the adage of the 'dog eat dog' world. The Mumbai Police force is the only one of its kind in the country which is inimical to their own tribesmen. This was evident even during the fallout of the infamous A.K. Telgi counterfeit stamp paper case where investigators arrested not just junior level police inspectors but even the then police commissioner, joint commissioner, DCP and a few ministers. When compared to the series of catastrophic arrests of senior officers in Telgi case, this was a much smaller matter, though Sharma was an important stalwart than those prosecuted unfairly earlier.

As per the rule, Sharma was produced at court and remanded to seven days of police custody. The administration wanted to chastise him severely by covering his head with a veil while being herded to court. Inspector George staunchly resisted the need for such action.

'Sir, this burkha is meant for those criminals who need to be identified,' George had reportedly said.

'Who does not know Sharma's face in the city! Secondly, I will not heap that humiliation on my own colleague.'

George took a similar stance when some officers wanted to throw Sharma into the lock up along with petty criminals. He ensured that Sharma was escorted to a cabin in the police station itself. Ironically, Sharma, who was remanded to police custody under the pretext of further investigations, was not interrogated even once while he was in the Bandra Police detention.

A week after biding his time in that cabin as an accused, Sharma was then sent to Thane Central Jail. Going to jail shattered Sharma emotionally. The prison was full of his enemies. Many criminals were serving their time there as a result of Sharma's actions as a police officer. Many others were friends or relatives of those he had killed in encounters. Sharma knew that surviving such enemies in Thane Jail would be his biggest challenge so far.

Perhaps, he would have thought if rebelling against his father to join the police force had been worth it.

4

Making of the Class of 83

It was almost night. The sound of muted thuds echoed softly in the parade ground at the Police Training College (PTC) in Nashik as the two cadets marched up and down its length in perfect coordination. A few others hung around to watch, but most of the cadets in the batch were used to the spectacle by now.

'Are you regretting this yet?' Vijay asked.

'Do I ever?' Pradeep shot back as they did an about-turn and started on another lap of the ground.

Now known as the Maharashtra Police Academy (MPA), the institute for trainee police officers started off as the Police Training School in Pune in 1906 under the British raj. It was shifted to Nashik in 1908 and renamed the PTC in 1961 after the state of Maharashtra was formed. It was subsequently renamed again as the MPA and was given autonomous status by the state government in 2016.

The MPA provides comprehensive academic and physical training to SIs and deputy superintendents. Once, it was also the training ground for officers of the Bombay Province—present day Gujarat, Sindh and parts of Karnataka—before the Central Police Training College at Mount Abu was founded in 1948.

Cadets from several other states, too, are brought to the MPA for crash courses in various subjects. Over the years, the MPA has been equipped with state-of-the-art forensic and cyber laboratories so that cadets can be trained in the latest aspects of investigations.

All of twenty years, Pradeep Sharma was among a few chosen young men who had started their training at PTC in March 1983. The son of a college professor working in Dhule in Maharashtra, Sharma developed the ambition to become a police officer at a very young age.

Sharma's career choice was influenced in no small measure by his father's profession and intimidating presence. Professor Rameshwar Sharma would leave for college by 7 a.m., return by 11 a.m., take a nap for two hours, have his evening tea at 4 p.m., step out of the house at 7 p.m., return in an hour, revise his teaching plan for the next day and would be asleep by 9.30 p.m. It was a set routine that Sharma failed to comprehend and could not imagine adopting.

The other factor was his neighbour, a police officer who exuded an aura of glamour that was only seen in Hindi movies back in the day. Every morning, around 11.30 a.m., a young Sharma, who was still in college at the time, would step out of his house to watch the officer leave for work on his motorcycle, clad in khaki uniform and sporting black sunglasses which were associated with a policeman even then.

The same officer, Dilip Pagar, also influenced Sharma's career choice in another way. Pagar's father was a public prosecutor and taught law at a local college. Sharma attended many of his lectures as a teenager, and slowly, he developed an interest in crime, punishment and all things in between. He also began craving the honour and prestige that came with being a policeman.

Professor Sharma, who was the strictest of disciplinarians, not only drove his son away from academics but also unwittingly fostered the spirit of rebellion in Pradeep Shama. The professor had a clear definition of right and wrong, while Sharma never conformed with his ideas. Sharma even contested in college elections without his father's knowledge. Because for his father, only goons stood for college elections.

Even though he did it covertly, Sharma did it in style. During his first year of master's in science, Organic Chemistry, he decided to run for University Representative (UR). The post was a coveted one and Sharma knew he would have to put in some real effort in order to win the election.

Sharma's university was also attended by many students from other states who stayed at the university hostel. Sharma knew that while the local students would vote for him, the outsiders would be a problem. He thought long and hard about this, and finally came up with a plan.

On the eve of voting day, Sharma bought tickets to a movie for all the outsider students—thirty-one in all. He purposely booked a 9 p.m. to 12 a.m. show and told them to have fun. The students happily filed into the theatre and lost themselves in the cinematic escape for three hours.

When they came out of the theatre, however, a surprise awaited them. A large tempo was parked right at the exit. Sharma was standing at its tailgate, while two of his burliest friends were leaning casually on either side.

'Get in, we are getting a lift to the hostel,' was all Sharma said and his two friends shuffled forward menacingly. The intimidated students had no idea what was happening, but they noticed that there were more of Sharma friends around the tempo and the theatre. Not wanting to take any chances in a strange city, they meekly boarded the tempo, which sped towards the outskirts of Dhule in the dead of the night.

An hour's drive later, the tempo came to a halt outside a farmhouse belonging to one of Sharma's friends. He opened the tailgate and smilingly led the students inside.

'Surprise!' he said. The group entered the house to find tables laden with food and drink. 'Have fun, boys. All on me,' he added, patting a couple of them on their shoulders.

The confused students milled about hesitantly at first, but hunger eventually got the better of them. Soon, they were merrily eating and drinking. Sharma quickly got onto a bike and sped back home.

The next morning, every outsider student who might not have voted for Sharma was happily sprawled out in the farmhouse, fast asleep. Everyone else knew Sharma, either personally or because he was the English professor's son. Sharma won in a landslide victory.

In the same week, Sharma mentioned his feat to a police constable in the area while they were working out together at the local gym. The constable listened to Sharma boast about it with increasing anger and disbelief before speaking.

'You idiot!' he hissed, looking around. 'Don't ever mention this to anyone ever again!'

'What? Why?' a confused Sharma asked.

'Because it might have been fun and games to you, but the law looks at it as kidnapping. There is a proper section in the Indian Penal Code for your little adventure!'

Sharma was speechless with shock.

The same year, his father took his mother, elder brother and sister to Uttar Pradesh, their home, for the summer vacations, paving way for Sharma to achieve his aspirations. As Sharma was studying the sciences, his vacations were starting later. As soon as his father was gone, Sharma went to the college librarian and sought his help.

'I want to study to become a policeman and the selection exam is in two months,' he told the librarian, who obliged by recommending scores of books on each subject in the exams.

For the next two months, with his family blissfully unaware, Sharma studied hard for eight to ten hours a day. He went on to appear for the Maharashtra Public Service Commission where he appeared for exams for both level of officers—deputy superintendent (DSP) as well as police sub inspector (PSI). The results for PSI came first and he cleared all subjects at the first attempt; the results for DSP had been delayed. Sharma was officially eligible to be a PSI.

Sharma was in a quandary about whether he should wait for the DSP results before starting the procedure for selection and other formalities for the post of PSI. However, the entire process would take several more months and in a village like Dhule in the early 1980s, becoming a SI was a massive feat. Plus, Sharma was getting increasingly stifled in his current life that was filled with rules and strict routines. He made his choice. He had to get out. At the time, designation and rank did not matter to him; much later, it was something he would regret. For Sharma, donning the khaki uniform was a glamourous affair and he would also be able to get away from his father.

When Sharma first told his parents about his decision, they were not supportive at all. His father particularly said it was a stupid idea and that the biggest goons were those who wore uniforms. For months, his father did not speak to him. Sharma had to put in some effort to convince them. Ultimately, they decided that it was his life and that he had the right to choose how he was going to live it.

And so, on 1 March 1983, Sharma found himself entering the PTC campus to become part of the famous—or infamous, depending on who was talking—batch of 83. The batch produced some of the most prolific, or notorious, 'encounter specialists' in the history of the Mumbai Police. The list includes Vijay Salaskar, Praful Bhosale, Aslam Momin and Ravindra Angre, all of them known for their kills in the 1990s, when the police force waged war against the underworld.

According to veteran crime branch officer, Shankar Kamble, the batch did exceedingly well because of their principal, Arvind Inamdar—a rare and highly competent IPS officer—who was shunted to an administrative posting. However, Inamdar decided to put his heart to the new recruits and gave his best to the batch which went on to become legendary in police history.

The training period was eventful under the able guidance of Arvind Inamdar, who retired as Director General of Police (DGP), Maharashtra. Inamdar was the principal of PTC at the time, and several graduates of the batch of 83 still swear by his name.

Known throughout the ranks as a no-nonsense officer, Inamdar tried to shape his students in his mould. A stickler for rules, Inamdar had no patience for mischief. Sharma and Salaskar were always at the receiving end of his wrath.

Sharma made many friends during his eleven months at PTC. Vijay Salaskar, a Maharashtrian, and Sharma, a north Indian from Agra—both as different as chalk and cheese—stood out in the batch. Yet they had plenty in common.

Both were extremely focussed and dedicated. They could have chosen any other calling if they wanted, but they were obsessed with the uniform and the idea of becoming a law enforcer. They soon became thick as thieves, much to everyone's chagrin. Especially because they didn't believe all that much in rules. Often, when Inamdar took a surprise roll call in the evening, the two young cadets would be missing, having sneaked out to watch a movie, grab their favourite meal or just to simply take a stroll. The misdemeanour would be met with strict punishment, such as marching up and down the parade ground for hours.

Both the young men, however, shared a carefree nature and a devil-may-care attitude. In the eleven months that they trained together, they got caught sneaking out at least seventeen to eighteen times.

While not exactly at the bottom, they had little interest in topping the class. That was for the likes of Sunil Brahme, who graduated at the top of the class and was awarded the Sword of Honour. The running myth at the time was that whoever got the Sword would get suspended soon after starting his career. Brahme, however, broke the myth when he took up voluntary retirement.

While the Brahmes of the batch focused on topping the class, Sharma and Salaskar quickly found something of their interest—firing lessons. It was something the two young men immensely enjoyed more than their batchmates. As it turned out, they were also quite good at it.

Unlike Salaskar who had never held a gun, Sharma had quite a firing practice during his teenage years.

At age thirteen, when Sharma would visit his uncle's place during his summer vacation, he would be sent off to guard the farm at night. His uncle's four sons were tasked with sleeping at the farm every night in order to discourage thefts. Every evening, they would set out for the farms with a box containing their dinner and a handbag containing a *katta* (country made revolver) and four rounds.

Sharma could never forget the feeling of handling the katta for first time in his small hands. In the by-lanes of Uttar Pradesh, kattas are made in every second household. Those with more time and resources on their hands make a living out of it.

In the late seventies, kattas were a simple affair, put together on a lathe machine. They would consist of a barrel and a basic trigger mechanism, and each round had to be loaded into the barrel separately.

Feeling the weight of the gun in his hands, Pradeep was aware of a slight tremor in his hand as he raised the katta above his head.

'Just fire with confidence whenever you are ready,' were the first firing lessons imparted by his cousin.

Pradeep took a deep breath, steadied his hand and fired. The shot reverberated across the empty land around them and was answered by the sound of dozens of birds taking flight from their perches on the myriad trees all around.

It had been over forty-five years since he had first fired a shot, and Sharma had not forgotten the feeling of exhilaration.

For the two months of his vacation, Sharma fired two rounds every night, gaining experience and steadiness in his hands. The idea of firing two rounds was to send out a message that the farm was not empty, and that the guards are well armed. The exercise would be repeated early in the morning, and the boys would leave once the workers arrived.

Years after Sharma's first experience in the farm, when he felt the real gun in his hand, he was immeasurably excited. Sharma felt euphoric and fired a volley of bullets. The trainer raised his eyebrows and shot Sharma a weird look before passing on the gun to Salaskar who remained calm and calculated when taking the shots.

Neither of the two friends had an inkling during their training that they would both become household names across Mumbai.

On that winter evening in 1983, having been caught sneaking out yet again, they were simply Pradeep and Vijay, two cadets out of the 450 in the class of 83.

5

Sensational Salaskar

Malad, Mumbai 1984

Traffic moved at a steady pace through the busy Malwani junction. SI Vijay Salaskar was leaning against his stationary motorbike which he had parked at a peculiar point along the road. Posters from a Bollywood movie were plastered on the wall behind him. In the adjacent lane, children from the nearby slums enjoyed a game of street cricket. He heard the cracking sound of their willow hitting a rubber ball, and then their vociferous appeals for a catch. The shade and bulk of a nearby tree hid his presence. But strategically, his position had laid out a clear view of the incoming traffic.

For the last hour, he had diligently watched white Ambassador cars and Chetak scooters drive past him but now the first signs of impatience were beginning to show. Salaskar tapped his foot fervently. Even after an excruciating wait, he had not spotted the man he'd come hunting for. He was on the lookout for Raja Shahabuddin, a notorious criminal from Malad who had cases of rape and murder against him.

Shahabuddin had established a stronghold in the Malwani area. He had no fear of the law. No policeman had ever managed to arrest him despite his gruesome criminal record. If anything, the cops preferred not to cross paths with him for Shahabuddin had scant respect for the khaki uniform.

And this was Salaskar's first year of posting. Still a rookie, he'd shown the will to go after a dangerous man like Shahabuddin. Perhaps, Salaskar knew he held an advantage of territory over his rival. Vijay was a local lad who had grown up in the lanes of Malad and returned as a cop there after his PTC training at Nashik.

That day, Salaskar had a reliable tip that Shahabuddin would visit the area around this hour. But despite waiting most of the afternoon, his quarry had not showed up. He was about to leave his spot thinking that either his informers had messed up or the criminal had managed to stay a step ahead of him and given him the slip.

Purely out of chance, Salaskar cast one last glance at the busy road. And there he was, Raja Shahabuddin riding atop his two-wheeler like he was the area's raja. He was driving in Salaskar's direction. Salaskar readied to spring upon Shahabuddin at the right moment. But then, he was still learning the art of policing and his excited movements gave his position away.

Shahabuddin saw Salaskar and must have been immediately reminded of the warning that the newly posted 'Saab was looking out for him like a hawk'. Shahabuddin was startled as if he had sighted a ghost, he turned his wrist on his bike's accelerator and spun it around. He sped off in the opposite direction, cutting his way through oncoming traffic.

Salaskar cussed. 'Stop!' he shouted. 'Stop right now.'

But Shahabuddin was not the kind of man who would obey an officer of the law. Salaskar saw the criminal's head vanish in the traffic. He could not afford to let Shahabuddin get away. He moved his vehicle off the side-stand, mounted the bike and kicked it to a start. And then, he was in the chase. Salaskar was leaning left and right, edging past cars and bikes and jaywalking pedestrians.

A few constables on the beat noticed Salaskar's chase and they too began following him.

A determined Salaskar did not notice that he was being followed by his own men. Soon, the dreaded Shahabuddin was back in Salaskar's sights. Once again, Salaskar shouted out for the gangster to stop and surrender.

For both the bikers it was a matter of reputation; while Shahabuddin did not want to get arrested by a rookie cop, Salaskar was loathe to return without netting him. It would be a major failure for him, he thought. Much was at stake for the hunter and the hunted.

Unlike Pradeep Sharma who was an outsider to Mumbai, Vijay Salaskar was very much the local boy. Salaskar was familiar with the Malwani area even before he had joined the force. It was 'his area' in many ways. He had studied at Dalmia College in the suburbs and completed his master's in commerce from Mumbai University.

Incidentally, Salaskar decided to pursue a career in law enforcement due to a run-in with the law. As a student of commerce, and the youngest among four siblings, Salaskar wanted to work for a bank and was preparing for its exams. But on an ordinary day in his young life, while he was boarding a crowded bus in Mumbai, Salaskar happened to brush his arm against a man ahead of him. It wasn't intentional but the man picked up a fight with Salaskar. What began as an exchange of words quickly escalated. Soon, the two men were nose to nose, thumping their chests against each other's, their hands balled into fists.

A patrolling havaldar noticed the ruckus. The cop broke up the impending fight and both men were hauled to the police station for creating a nuisance on the roads.

At the police station, Salaskar saw his rival flaunt his political connections. The man dropped names of local politicians and their visiting cards. He threatened the cops with dire consequences if they detained him any longer. Soon enough, the man was let go.

But Salaskar was made to wait at the police station for a long time. He had no connections to boast of. Salaskar had recently switched jobs from an administrator in a shipping company to junior officer in New India Assurance company. He had no clout. He kept pleading with the cops to hear his side of the story, but they plainly ignored him. Only when the policemen were satisfied that Salaskar had learnt a lesson, they let him go. On that fateful day, Vijay Salaskar understood the magnitude of power and the influence of political connections. Power was essential for survival in this city.

Salaskar began working his way towards attaining such power. He joined the Shiv Sena, a political party with roots in Maharashtra; their political plank is to further the agenda of the Marathi *Manoos* (Maharashtrian Man). Migrant workers from other states often found themselves at the receiving end of the Sena's ire for allegedly hogging a bulk of the city's employment avenues and leaving little for the local populace. But more than this anti-migratory stance, Salaskar was attracted to the power that came along with politics rather than politics itself. He soon rose to the position of a deputy *shakha pramukh* (locality leader) at a very young age.

An advertisement in a Marathi daily drew his attention towards police recruitment.

When the shakha veterans egged him to join the force, Salaskar felt that it was his best opportunity to get ahead in life. The day he was made to wait at the police station remained etched in his memory. Finally, he decided to pursue a career in the police forces for the power and authority of the position. He successfully passed the written exams and the physical tests. And after the batch of 83 graduated from PTC in Nashik, Salaskar was sent to Malad for his first posting in 1984. It was a homecoming of sorts.

On his home turf, Salaskar initially did quite well. One of his first major detections at Malad was a hit-and-run case. He had solved the case in less than twenty-four hours by using his contacts in the Road Transport Office (RTO) to trace the vehicle's owner who had committed the crime. Salaskar's fluency in language and his impeccable knowledge about the way city functioned came in handy. While he was revelling in the accolades he received for solving the hit-and-run, his senior at the police station threw him a significantly greater challenge.

'Vijay, a hit-and-run is not a big deal,' the senior said. '*Dum hai to Shahabuddin ko pakad ke dikha* (If you really have the guts, arrest Shahabuddin).'

Salaskar knew his senior's words were not meant to belittle his achievement but were a way of putting him onto bigger cases. He took the dare in the right spirit. Never one to back down from a formidable challenge, Salaskar set off on the quest to end Shahabuddin's reign of terror. He began scouring the area for leads, meeting with locals and his sources. His local advantage came into play. Information was forthcoming when he sought it.

But then Shahabuddin also had his own sources. He soon received word that Vijay Salaskar, the new cop in town, was actively looking out for him. This made him wary and he went underground.

Salaskar was happy to play the waiting game. He only had to wait for Shahabuddin to make a mistake. And Salaskar was known to be cool headed since his days at the academy. He bided his time and subsequently, Shahabuddin's fear mellowed. He felt that the rookie cop had given up the trail and planned a visit to his stronghold in Malwani. That proved to be his undoing.

Salaskar's informers were keeping track of Shahabuddin's movements and tipped him off about the planned visit. And thus, Salaskar had ended up at the busy junction to bring an end to this game of hide and seek.

As Salaskar snaked his way against the traffic, the only thought on his mind was to stop Raja Shahabuddin from escaping the clutches of the law again. Luck ran out on Shahabuddin when an accident ahead blocked the road just as he was about to take a sharp turn and go over to the opposite side.

Shahabuddin realized that he was trapped. But the gangster was not ready to give up yet. He dropped his bike on the road and began to flee on foot. Salaskar too continued the chase and began running after Shahabuddin. The entire street was now jam packed with traffic. The burly Shahabuddin had not run for long when he began to slow down. He put his hands on his knees, gasping for breath.

Salaskar thought the chase was over. He approached Shahabuddin to arrest him. But the criminal had other plans.

He turned and pulled out a gun from his pants. Salaskar was quick to draw too. The muscles of his hands responded from a trained memory. He reached for the gun in his holster. His right arm came out with the weapon, slightly bent. Three fingers were firmly folded around the grip. One finger supported the side of the frame. And then his left hand wrapped around his right and his thumbs were aligned. The butt of the weapon was firm and familiar in the flesh of his palm.

His forefinger squeezed the trigger. Hours of practice at the PTC shooting range had moulded him into a sharpshooter. He fired. And his training did not fail him. Three bullets whizzed through the air and hit Shahabuddin in the chest even before he could take proper aim at Salaskar. Shahabuddin fell.

Salaskar heard terrified screams from the crowd that had just witnessed an encounter. Families in cars rolled up the windows and huddled for safety. Few onlookers ran helter-skelter. Salaskar lowered his weapon and approached Shahabuddin's immobile body. Salaskar's breathing eased when he realized that the gangster had been eliminated. Shahabuddin's mouth was agape. Eyes open. Head titled. A stream of blood poured out of Shahabuddin's body and spilled onto the tar road. The shootout in a busy street had ended without loss to public life or property.

Salaskar's senior officer was pleased that a young cop had responded to the challenge of bringing a dreaded gangster to task. Salaskar's bravery also earned him the local population's appreciation; they already knew him as their own. But the most critical lesson he learnt was to understand the importance of a good information network.

He would not have been able to obtain such accurate intel on Shahabuddin had it not been for his informants. Not only was he able to track an elusive criminal he was also aware of his exact movements around a given hour. This encounter marked Salaskar for early advancement in the force.

In the first year of his service, SI Vijay Salaskar had proved that his mettle belonged to the mould that required to fight far greater battles for the Mumbai Police.

6

Sharma's Kindergarten—Mahim

Near the end of his training period, every police recruit is consumed by a single concern: his first posting.

Each policeman has his own ideas and expectations. Some want to serve in or around their hometowns to be near their families. Some hope to get posted in conflict zones like Naxalite areas, where risk is paralleled only by accolades. And yet, there are others who want 'cream' postings where money and influence can be accumulated in little time and in large quantities.

In the late 1980s, there was only one destination of choice for ambitious, young policemen: Mumbai.

The underworld in Mumbai at the time was flourishing with extortion rackets. Gangsters like Karim Lala, Babu Reshim and Rajan Nair, also known as Bada Rajan, were waging war against each other to establish their supremacy over the city. The Pathan gangs and Dawood Ibrahim were also locked in a violent battle. Blood spilled freely on the Mumbai streets. Contract killings were the order of the day.

The citizens were getting restless, and the police were getting desperate.

Just a year before the batch of 83 graduated from MPA at Nashik, Mumbai had witnessed its first encounter killing. Manohar Surve, alias Manya, a young resident of Dadar who went from being a college class topper to a dreaded dacoit, had been gunned down in Wadala on 11 January 1982. Manya, among the few educated members of the underworld, had managed to hold his own in the city for two years despite organized crime gangs springing up all around him. In fact, Manya not only stood his ground but also hit back. In 1981, Sabir Ibrahim Kaskar's murder, the elder brother of Dawood Ibrahim Kaskar, was plotted by Manya.

Crime experts and police officers dispute Manya's involvement in the killing. However, there are different versions of the murder. After this incident, Manya became a marked man. A team comprising Police Inspector Isaac Samson and SIs Ishaque Bagwan, Raja Tambat and Sanjay Parande laid a trap for Manya near Ambedkar College in Wadala. Bagwan and Tambat shot Manya five times. Manya died while being rushed to Sion Hospital, spewing curses at the policemen who had pumped bullets into him.

Out of 450 cadets in the 83 batch, around ninety were posted in Mumbai. To Sharma's supreme disappointment, his first posting was with the Airport Police Station in the western suburbs. The Airport Police Station was formed primarily to take care of matters pertaining to the domestic terminal (now known as Chhatrapati Shivaji International Airport). The occasional accident or murder in its jurisdiction extends a little beyond the domestic terminal's boundaries.

In a city ripe with opportunity, the Airport Police Station was hardly a worthy posting. Even Sharma's reporting head at the time realized that this was a colossal waste of Sharma's talent and abilities. Sharma was advised to ask for another posting. With some trepidation, Sharma approached Julio Ribeiro, then Commissioner of Police, and expressed his concerns. Ribeiro's strong persona and aura flummoxed the rookie officer.

'Why do you want to change your posting?' Ribeiro curtly asked Sharma.

Sharma gathered his wits and blurted out an answer. 'Sir, I came to Mumbai to fight organized crime,' he said, haltingly. 'Here I am only watching the airport visitors.'

Ribeiro glanced sharply at Sharma, measuring the intensity of Sharma's sincerity and intentions. Then Ribeiro bent towards his desk and scribbled something on a file which Sharma could not comprehend until days later when he received a letter. To Sharma's relief, Ribeiro had not only agreed to the change but also posted him close to Sharma's bachelor quarters in Bandra, also known as the queen of the suburbs.

And so, on the fifteenth day of his service, Sharma reported to Senior PI Ismail Rajguru in charge of the Mahim Police Station—one of the most 'active spots' as far as the underworld or organized crime is concerned. Rajguru was the next to use his X-ray eyes to scan Sharma's bubbling enthusiasm. Although a greenhorn, Rajguru had a hunch that if groomed properly, Sharma would go on to establish a stellar career. Sharma remembers Rajguru as a 'good man' who was very supportive and taught him a lot.

Mahim is still classified as a 'communally sensitive' area—cop speak for areas where members of the Muslim community reside in large numbers—due to the Makhdoom Ali Mahimi Dargah, commonly known as the Mahim dargah. The priority for any cop posted at Mahim is to have as many eyes and ears on the ground as possible.

Thus, Sharma's first lesson on the job was the backbone of policing: gathering informants.

Also referred to as 'human intelligence' by elite officers and agencies and as the '*khabri* (informant) network' by the grassroots, the informant network is the strength of every police force in the world. Policemen, while admitting the advantages of technology like CCTV cameras, cellular location mapping, DNA tests and forensic analysis, will never stop swearing by their informants. Some of the biggest cases have been solved and the most serious crimes prevented because of tip offs provided by the informant network which is almost an institution.

Rajguru gave Sharma a police van and two constables who were well versed in policing as well as familiar with the Mahim jurisdiction. But Sharma had to learn to fish for himself.

'Go out in the field and build your own information network,' Rajguru said.

Sharma started small. Pickpocketing was rampant on the streets at the time. Fast-moving, light-fingered pickpockets found a ready supply of wallets to be stolen on the crowded streets around the dargah. Unsuspecting devotees and pedestrians would find their pockets lighter long after the pickpocket had weaved his way through the dense crowd and disappeared into the shady lanes of Mahim. Scores of complaints were lodged every day.

Under Rajguru's guidance, Sharma's quest began with picking up all the history sheeters in the area known to pick pockets for a living. The pickpockets had demarcated their areas of operation so that they could work without disrupting each other's flow of income—a symbiotic system of survival that exists even today. With the help of the constables, Sharma matched names of the suspects to their areas. Then, he went after all of them.

He began with one man, and that one man led Sharma to four others, who in turn led him to ten others. With each suspect that he picked up, Sharma put to action all the theoretical knowledge about interrogation that he had learnt, identifying when to use force and when to use skill. Soon, he had results. The suspects started confessing and Sharma could place them under arrest, solving cases and earning a reputation for himself.

Every night, Sharma would make detailed notes in his diary about the people he had arrested, the ones he still had to, the number of cases against each one, known associates, modus operandi, area of operations and every other detail. The word of his diary spread among the history sheeters. On the streets of Mahim, the average pickpocket shivered at the thought of his name cropping up in Sharma's dreaded diary.

Sharma's day at work often extended beyond fourteen hours. In a span of three months, he put sixty to seventy pickpockets behind bars. Information kept pouring in and Sharma's interest deepened.

It wasn't long before the suspects started doubling up as informants. The first few strands of Sharma's informant network, which later grew to enviable proportions, started taking shape. Trusting his instinct, Sharma took three to four pickpockets under his wing, adopting the 'good cop' attitude with them, taking care of their small needs and assuring them protection as long as they helped him in return. The pickpockets were only too happy to pass on whatever they gathered through their own network in exchange for leniency and other benefits. Soon, Sharma knew who to turn to every time a big theft occurred in the Mahim police's jurisdiction.

Policemen across the globe will agree that informants have different motivations. There are a few, although only few, who genuinely want to play their part in fighting crime in their respective areas and are also able to pick up the local grapevine, which they then pass on to policemen they trust.

Others do it to put their rivals out of business, and while the police know this, they are fine with it if it keeps the crime graph in check. Yet others do it for good, old-fashioned reasons like money.

When he was not busy turning suspects into sources, Sharma was also out on the streets. Watching. Listening. Absorbing. Sometimes, he would break up a fight before it escalated. At other times, he would intervene in local disputes and ensure law and order was maintained. Through all of this, he constantly made new friends and invested time and energy into broadening his network.

Sharma did not know that these seemingly trivial acts would one day manifest into bigger successes, and he would soon reap the first fruit of his labour.

7

The Outsider's Onslaught

Sharma's biggest challenge in Mumbai was that he was an outsider. He did not know how the city functioned. He had come to this big bad city from the back and beyond of Dhule because he had desperately wanted to escape his authoritarian and non-comprising disciplinarian father. And now that he was here, he needed to work out how he was going to make it in this city because he was not going to return to his people until he had done so.

His father had given him Rs 2500 and packed him off to Mumbai. Now, Sharma was entirely on his own. But Sharma's money ran out in no time and he was soon borrowing money from his colleagues to remain in the city.

Sharma remembers his initial days of struggle in Mahim as a mixture of hard-work and fun. As there were a lot of formalities to complete, Sharma didn't get his salary for the first two months. When the paperwork was finally done, he got three months' pay in one go. For the first time, Sharma knew what it felt like to be rich.

The first thing he did was buy a motorbike—a Bullet Enfield—like the one he had seen PI Pagar drive back in Dhule.

Sharma started patrolling his entire jurisdiction astride the Bullet, aviator sunglasses perched on his nose. Saving money was a concept he was not yet familiar with, and he did not even have a bank account back then. All the money he made would go under his mattress, although he often spent more than he saved.

Apart from the assignments given by his senior, Ismail Rajguru, Sharma would spend his days riding around and making it known that he was always watching his people.

His own constables were of great help to him. Every police station has at least one constable with greying hair and experience worth decades under it, and these constables are often the unofficial consultants at the police station. They are affectionately known by many names, including 'Master', 'Bapu' and 'Guruji', and everyone, from the senior PI downwards, turns to them when in doubt.

These constables, who start their career at the lowest rung of the force, have put in unbelievable number of hours mingling with the people in their areas, understanding their problems and officially or unofficially helping them. They have sat with the people at their evening hang outs, broken bread with them in religious functions and danced with hearty abandon at their weddings. The local constable might not have as much position as an officer, but he is second to none when it comes to influence and love of the people.

Consequently, it is the constable who gets the best tip offs, many a times without even asking for them. The people who have seen these constables try to idolize them; they trust these constables more than some aviator-wearing, handlebar moustache-sporting officer. Many citizens provide these tip offs without expecting any kind of reward in return. The constables, in turn, remember everyone who has helped them, and make sure they return the favour in any way possible.

There are legendary stories about the constables and their amazing resourcefulness in the department. The old timers still remember the triumvirate of Pandu Hawaldar, Constable number 303 and Ibrahim Hawaldar (Dawood Ibrahim's father). Whenever there was a complicated case, the trio would be summoned together for some important leads, and the *tigdi* (trio), as they were called, always managed to crack it in no time. Together, they shouldered the entire crime branch's burden against the many mafia outfits back in the day until Ibrahim Hawaldar was suspended and the other two retired and faded into oblivion.

One such constable, named Sayyed, was with the Mahim Police Station. He took a liking to the young Sharma and his drive, and soon the veteran and the rookie hit it off. Sayyed knew that Sharma was not from the city and needed handholding to learn the ropes of policing. His being an officer was just a matter of police protocol otherwise Sharma had all the respect for Sayyed.

That night, when Sharma was on nocturnal vigil and had nothing much to look at, Sayyed received a confirmed tip off while patrolling his beat and hurried back to the police station. Sharma was at the station house, looking through the station diary, when Sayyed walked in. Sharma looked up and gave him a little smile. He knew that look on Sayyed's face.

'What?'

'Two trucks from Mahim have been hired to go to Shivaji Park sea face and back. All of this happens tonight itself,' Sayyed said.

Sharma, who was still new, failed to comprehend the significance of the information, something that Sayyed's veteran mind had immediately picked up on.

Those were the days when smuggling was at its peak. Goods like electronics, gold and foreign made clothes were smuggled into the city at night and spirited away to *godown*s (storage spaces), after which the buyers would make a killing in the market. The smuggled goods were in huge demand in the city, and every sea face, including Shivaji Park, Mahim and Versova, had fixed landing points.

Ships on their way to nearby cities would make a quick detour to pre-decided landing points, where gangs of men would be waiting. These men would be hired on a contract basis and would work for any smugglers' ring if the pay was good. Their job was to wade into waist-deep water, pick up the smuggled goods from the ships, hurry back to the shore and load the goods into trucks. The faster the better. Those who worked fast and efficiently made a name for themselves and were sought after.

Sharma, however, hardly knew all of this, and failed to understand why two trucks being hired from Mahim to Shivaji Park was such a big deal.

Sayyed shook his head.

'Smuggling, sir! Smuggling. *Maal aa raha hai* (Goods are coming in),' he said.

Understanding the significance, Sharma immediately reached for the keys to his Bullet, asking Sayyed to hop on.

Ten minutes later, Sharma parked his bike in a lane near the sea face and he and Sayyed dismounted. Silently, they made their way, jogging from cover to cover, as close to the landing point as they dared. Their behaviour was quite filmy. Sharma had neither alerted his seniors as most of them would be sleeping nor had he sought any back up from the police station. Like the filmy cops he decided to take the smugglers on single-handedly.

This had proved too costly to him later and would serve as an unforgettable lesson for him.

After around a fifteen-minute wait, Sharma and Sayyed noticed the lights of a ship approaching at a distance. At the same time, there was movement on the beach. Through the pitch black of the night, the two policemen could make out the dim shapes of two trucks parked in one corner, and some smaller shapes, which they assumed to be the loaders, milling around.

They waited till the loaders had picked up the crates of goods and reached the shore before moving in. Smugglers in those days had one more thing to worry about apart from policemen. There were gangs that specialized in robbing consignments that landed at sea faces. The gangs would wait patiently till the goods had come to the shore and then descend in large numbers, attacking the loaders from all sides. Once the loaders had run away, the robbers would take the goods, often in the trucks hired by the loaders themselves, and sell the goods on the black market. It was easy money and there were landings almost every night, which made the racket a very lucrative one.

As a result, the loaders started taking measures to protect themselves. Those that could afford it started carrying guns. In other instances, the smugglers themselves provided armed guards. In most cases, however, the loaders simply armed themselves with stones in case of an attack.

As the loaders started wading back to the shore, crates of smuggled goods in their hands, Sharma drew his service revolver from his hip holster. Together, he and Sayyed walked as stealthily as they could till cover ran out. Then they both straightened and advanced.

'Stop!' Sharma called out. '*Koi hilneka nahi! Maal neeche rakh!* (No one move! Put the goods down!)'

In the dark of the night, the loaders mistook Sharma and Sayyed, both dressed in civilian clothes, for robbers. Almost as one, they all dropped their crates, whipped out stones from their pockets and started throwing it at them.

It was quite a shower of stones. Neither Sharma nor Sayyed were prepared for this. Ducking amid a hail of stones, Sharma swore and raised his gun. He fired blindly into the crowd. This was first time Sharma had ever fired from his service revolver in 1985.

The shooting had quite an impact on the unarmed men. The loaders dropped the crates, abandoned the trucks and ran for their lives. Thus, all of them managed to decamp from the scene. Sharma and Sayyed ran forward and found the sea face empty. Sharma could not help feeling a little disappointed. It was the first shot he had fired on the job, and he had failed to hit anyone. He also did not manage any arrests.

As per procedure, he called the police inspector in charge of the night shift at the police station, who sent a team to conduct a *panchnama* (spot report) and other formalities. The smuggled goods were carefully inventoried and then taken to the police station, where Sharma filed a complaint against unidentified persons for smuggling and hindering a public servant from discharging his duty.

It was dawn by the time all the paperwork was done. Sharma was living in Andheri at the time. However, he was simply too tired to make the journey and instead went up to the first floor of the police station and made his way to a room where he would frequently sleep after his night shifts. The goods seized a few hours ago, too, had been dumped there and Sharma soon fell asleep surrounded by video cassette players and gaberdine trousers.

It was late morning when a constable came to wake him up with a glass of cutting chai in his hands.

'Senior saheb wants to see you,' the constable told Sharma as he handed him the tea.

Shaking off his sleep, Sharma freshened up, put on a spare shirt that he would keep in the police station and went down to the senior PI's cabin.

Ismail Rajguru was signing one of the scores of papers he would sign that day when Sharma entered his office and saluted smartly. Rajguru let Sharma stand at attention for a minute before turning his attention to him. Rajguru had never scolded Sharma until then.

'Do you know what you have done, Pradeep?' he asked.

'Sir?' was all Sharma said. He knew a trick question when he heard one.

'Do you have any idea what you have done?' Rajguru snapped.

This time, Sharma asked, 'What is wrong, sir?'

'What is wrong,' Rajguru said, his voice rising, 'is that I have a young man in his twenties with a bullet wound to his thigh admitted to Hinduja hospital. And what is even worse is that the wound was caused by a police issue bullet!'

Sharma didn't know what to say. For one absurd moment, he was almost happy that his bullet had hit someone after all.

'Who told you to go out there guns blazing?' Rajguru asked furiously. 'Whose permission did you take before you opened fire?'

'But sir ... they were attacking us...'

'I don't care!' Rajguru snapped and raged on for another five minutes before dismissing Sharma.

The young cop walked out of his senior's cabin in a daze, undoing the top button of his shirt.

Around ten years down the line, when 'shoot first, seek permission later' became the norm, Sharma would often remember this day and think about how times had changed.

Instead of being applauded for foiling a major smuggling landing, he had been berated because of one bleeding man.

Fuming, Sharma decided to formulate his own rules and live by them.

8

Sharma Supremacy

Sharma moved with lightning speed even before the towering six-foot, stoutly built gangster in front of him could understand what was happening. Extending his hand behind the small of the gangster's back, Sharma pulled a gun out of his waistband and with equal agility, shoved the long barrel of the gun into the gangster's mouth, down to the opening of his throat.

The gangster's eyes reddened with pain and humiliation. He choked. For several long seconds, not a word was spoken between the two men of almost equal height, broad shoulders and a certain craziness in their demeanour. Sharma glared hard at Sarmast Khan. With his eyes, he signalled Khan to walk towards the road in the same position with the gun placed in his mouth.

Decades before tweeting to Sushma Swaraj, Minister of External Affairs (MEA), was an option for stranded Indians who needed assistance on foreign soil, hapless job-seekers from Mumbai who were sent abroad for supposedly well-paying jobs were among the biggest victims of fraud in the early eighties.

Self-styled recruitment agents would lure young men with the promise of high paying jobs in the Middle East.

An ever-inflating population and their need for employment resulted in hordes of jobseekers flocking to the offices of these agents. Jobs in the Middle East or working for gangs were fast becoming the only two choices for the unemployed middle-class youth in the eighties. Many parents pushed their sons towards the former option.

The manpower export 'offices' would be one or two room affairs packed into one of the many commercial complexes in Mahim. Two or three men would sit on cheap chairs with posters of scenic Middle Eastern locations lining the walls. Passports and visas would be processed within days with the help of the well-oiled machinery that works through 'agents' and the corrupt establishment. Tickets would be booked, and the job seekers would pay lakhs of rupees, hoping for high returns on their investments.

These young men, mainly Muslims, who were degree holders in engineering and architecture would be among the thousands pushed to desperation because there were too many graduates and not enough jobs. They would eagerly put their parents' life savings at stake believing that once they reached the Gulf, their parents would be wanting for nothing.

Instead, when they landed in Dubai or Qatar or Bahrain, they would be herded away in rickety vans to cheap accommodations and put to work as goat herders and cattle grazers. They would have no money and no way of contacting their families, and no access to the proper channels to seek help.

The only option was to suffer the hardship and the indignity till they had saved enough money for a one-way ticket back home. The lucky ones would then manage to escape from their workplaces, which bore striking resemblances to labour camps, and come back to India intending to confront the recruiting agents and demand their money back. Instead, the victims would be met by burly henchmen with revolvers, daring them to start an argument.

According to Sharma, there were around 400 to 500 such recruiting agencies in Mahim itself. As soon as the agents realized that their victims were figuring out ways to return to India, they would approach the gangs for protection in exchange for a price. The gangs, which got money as well as a reputation, were only too happy to oblige.

One such gangster who provided protection to recruiting agents was Sarmast Khan. A strapping young man in his late twenties, Khan was the son of a south Mumbai newspaper publisher and was part of the Pathan gang. Like his name, Sarmast was intoxicated with the power and fear he wielded on the hapless men around him. But fate had other plans for him.

Pradeep Sharma wanted to crack many cases and earn popularity and reputation in the area. To this end, he had expanded his horizons, moving on from pickpockets to recruiting agents, which was the biggest racket of the time. Sharma was still gathering intelligence on these rackets and figuring out his next step when one of his informers told him about Sarmast Khan, the particularly nasty gangster who swaggered around the lanes of Mahim with two revolvers on him.

As is the case with most bullies, Khan thrived on fear. His affiliation to the Pathan gang and the two imported revolvers he brandished discouraged anyone from crossing him or complaining to the police about him. Typically, it is always the informants who, behind the reassuring veil of secrecy, tip off the police about such characters.

For Sharma, Khan was literally begging to be made an example of. Sharma decided to tip the scales and do something extraordinary to not only shatter Khan's arrogance but also restore the confidence of general masses in the police machinery.

One afternoon, Sharma took a constable with him and visited the recruiting agent's office when the buildings and the lanes in the area were the most crowded. The timing was not a coincidence. Suddenly, Sharma noticed the strongly built Pathan.

'Are you Sarmast Khan?' Sharma asked the burly man at the door of the agent's office.

Sarmast Khan scoffed. 'What if I am?'

Khan's reply was among the most cliched in the history of crime flicks. It did not do him any favours. If there was one thing Sharma hated more than criminals, it was cocky criminals. Khan's kohl-lined eyes and his dour, scowling face would have intimidated any middle class white collared man. But Sharma's blood begun boiling with the silent rage of helplessness that he couldn't kill this man even though he was a suitable candidate for an encounter because the man had not attacked him.

Sharma thought of his cool-headed friend, Salaskar, who had displayed amazing gumption by gunning down a gangster in the first year of his first posting. Sharma decided to be different but decisive.

Before anyone could understand what was happening, Sharma's hand shot out and drew one of Khan's two revolvers from under his belt. A surprised Khan could only open his mouth in astonishment, and Sharma shoved the revolver's barrel into Khan's mouth even before Khan could utter a sound. After a long silence and staring match, Sharma broke the silence.

'*Bahot masti hai na tere andar*? (You have too much fun inside, right?)' Sharma breathed in the stupefied gangster's face. '*Chal, nikalta hoon* (Come, I'll take it out).'

Like any bully, Khan paled in the face of such fierce retaliation. Sharma caught him by his shirt collar and dragged him out of the building, and into the crowded street. Almost immediately, word started spreading as people pressed closer for a better look. Loud whispers emanated from the crowd.

'*Abey, woh dekh!* (Hey, look there!)'

'*Woh udhar dekh kya ho raha hai!* (Look at what's happening there!)'

'*Woh toh Sarmast Khan hai na?* (Isn't that Sarmast Khan?)'

'*Arrey yeh toh apne Sharma sahab hain!* (By God, this is our Sharma sahib!)'

'*O, saala! Uska hi ghoda ghusa diya sahab ne toh!* (Bloody hell! Sharma has put his gun into his mouth!)'

Instead of bundling him into the police jeep, Sharma trotted a sweating Khan with his own gun in his mouth to the police station which was almost half a kilometre away. A crowd of gleeful onlookers trailed behind Sharma. As they passed the main intersection of Mahim, past the Makhdoom Baba Dargah, it turned into a mini procession. Everyone thronged to witness the spectacle of the decade. People who could not see through the crowd presumed it to be some local leader's funeral procession. Little did they know it was the funeral of Sarmast's megalomania.

Word had reached the police station even before the little procession got there. All the fear that Sarmast Khan had drilled into the people's mind evaporated on that day.

Khan's arrest not only sealed Sharma's place in the hearts of the people of Mahim, it also opened a new avenue for him. Khan was a big catch. The police recovered four to five imported revolvers from him, which in those days was a big deal. He had some eighteen to twenty cases against him in various police stations, including Mahim, where he worked, and Nagpada, where he lived. Among other crimes, he was accused of snatching a policeman's rifle and firing rounds in the air during the 1984 riots.

Though Sharma didn't realize it at the time, Khan's arrest was going to put him on a path that would eventually make him famous. On that day, Sharma earned the blessings of scores of people and that too without firing a single bullet.

Khan's arrest earned Sharma a name not only in Mahim, but in the other parts of the city as well. His batchmates, and a few superiors, called to congratulate him. Officers started coming over to shake his hand and pat him on the shoulder, telling him to keep up the good work.

One compliment he received was from Emmanuel Amolik, an encounter specialist working with the crime branch at the time. Sharma was enforcing bandobast at a busy signal in Mahim one afternoon, not long after Khan's arrest, when Amolik came up to him on his motorcycle.

'*Uda kyon nahi diya*? (Why didn't you shoot him dead?)' Amolik asked Sharma. '*Ekdum fit customer tha* (He was a fit customer).'

'Fit customer' is police slang for an apt candidate for an encounter killing. After the Manya Surve encounter, when policemen realized that killing apt candidates would be rewarded with accolades instead of disciplinary action, every ambitious cop was on the lookout for 'fit customers'. Sharma feebly explained that he had arrested Khan because the latter had surrendered without a fight. Amolik just chuckled and congratulated Sharma on his achievement.

Sharma also started a new chapter of learning on the job. Being a foot soldier for Karim Lala, Khan turned out to be a treasure trove of information about the Mumbai gangs. During Sarmast Khan's interrogations, Sharma received his first tutorials on the Mumbai mafia. Sharma heard of Karim Lala and his Pathan gang. About Vardarajan Mudaliar and Haji Mastan Mirza. Dawood's and Sabir's war against the Pathans. Sabir's elimination. Dawood's retaliation. Anyone who could exact revenge by getting his rival killed in a busy courtroom, the way Dawood got Amirzada killed, was a big challenge for the Mumbai Police.

A rapt Sharma could only listen as Sarmast Khan narrated the Pathan gang's history and its activities while being interrogated in the lock up at the Mahim Police Station. Over innumerable glasses of cutting chai, Sharma grilled Khan till late into the night, amassing all the knowledge and taking notes in his diary. He started reading newspapers and comparing his notes with news reports, adding to his knowledge and building a picture of the Mumbai underworld in his mind.

The same way that he first went after pickpockets and the recruitment rackets, Sharma now set his sights on the underworld. He started picking up other lieutenants of various gangs named by Khan and squeezed them for every little sliver of information that they had to offer. Soon, Sharma hit upon an idea.

It was fashionable for foot soldiers of the underworld to carry guns with them, if only to show them off to their friends and their favourite bar dancers. Once Sharma started digging, he saw a pattern. Several bars in the city were the preferred hangouts for gang members, and these provided him with the opening he needed.

In the early hours of the morning, when most of the city was asleep, the gangsters would stumble out of their favourite bars, often owned by other gang members, after an entire night of debauchery. They would get into their plush cars, or pre-arranged taxis if they were too drunk, and rudely tell the drivers to drive them home.

Sharma set his plan in motion.

At strategic locations along the way, the gangsters' cars or taxis were stopped at *nakabandi*s (check posts) set up by the police. The gangsters were first confused and then furious. Who dared to stop them? they asked their drivers in slurring voices. Then the doors to their vehicles were wrenched open, and they were dragged out by the scruff of their necks. Squinting through the drunken haze, they found themselves staring into the grinning face of PSI Pradeep Sharma.

Sharma was riding on a huge crest of popularity. At the same time, he was also enjoying crushing the gang menace in his jurisdiction. Shattering the ego of a gangster like Sarmast Khan had sublimated Sharma's aspirations.

The most important lesson that Sharma had learnt was that more than the garbage, the city needed to be cleansed off the gangsters who plagued the streets. And only a fearless cop could do this.

Sharma set his eyes on the biggest and most powerful gang in the city: Dawood's D-Company.

He was raring to go for them.

9

The Dream Team

Across the world, members of the police force work on the 'buddy-pair' system in which two policemen form a partnership and pound the pavement together. In the US, partners are an official thing; a rookie is usually partnered with a veteran. After having gained experience, he, in turn, gets a rookie partner when the veteran retires. The idea is to blend energy with experience.

The buddy-pair system works on several principles, including mutual trust and understanding. A breach of any of these principles results in an almost irreparable fracture in the partnership. Policemen who are partners do everything together—legal or illegal—and go on to become family friends. One cop's wife trusts the other cop to guard her husband's life with his own, and vice versa.

In India, such an idea was never promulgated or implemented. However, the cops still formed unofficial partnerships with their peers and achieved several milestones together. Pradeep Sharma's first partner was Vijay Salaskar. They had developed a good rapport during their days in PTC in Nashik in 1983 where squads of ten used to be made based on surnames. As both their surnames began with 'S', the two young cops were placed in one squad. The buddy system instilled a sense of camaraderie between the two. They took the bouquets and the brickbats together, never letting each other down even in the face of PTC Principal Arvind Inamdar's strict punishments that he often put the duo through for their dislike of rules. Their love for shooting further drew them together. And their joy knew no bounds when both were posted in Mumbai after graduating from the PTC.

They had kept in touch with each other through their various postings across the city and helped each other out as and when it was needed, further strengthening their bond of friendship and trust.

Early in his career, when Sharma was posted at Mahim Police Station when his star was on the ascent, he had earned grudging admiration from his colleagues across the city. Salaskar too had lauded Sharma for his bravura with Sarmast Khan. On one of those days, Sharma was sitting at his desk and browsing through a file when Salaskar brought a fellow officer, Poojara, to meet Sharma. The tension on Poojara's face was palpable. Sharma shut the file and turned towards the men.

'What's wrong?' he asked, raising an eyebrow.

'Our batch mate Poojara has a peculiar problem,' Salaskar said. 'Perhaps, you can help him.' Then Salaskar patted Poojara on the back and pointed towards Sharma. 'Go on. Tell him.'

Poojara took a deep breath. 'I lost a box in an autorickshaw last night.'

Sharma slapped his thigh and laughed. 'So? You want me to file a police complaint?'

'I was on a patrol,' Poojara said. 'The box contained thirteen rounds of *sarkari* (government) ammunition.'

Patrolling in autorickshaws was a common sight back in the eighties when police vehicles were not available in plenty and had to be issued on priority basis. A young SI would always lose out to his seniors. As a result, the more enterprising of the rookies befriended autorickshaw drivers in their areas. In exchange for giving the officer a free ride of the area, the auto-driver got bragging rights about being close to the cops.

That night, Poojara had completed his patrol and got off the autorickshaw with his service revolver in its holster. However, he forgot about the extra ammunition that he had left in the backseat and didn't realize it till he had reached the police station. It took another couple of hours to track down the autorickshaw again. But by this time, the ammunition had disappeared.

Poojara knew he was in trouble. There would be hell to pay if his superiors discovered the huge blunder. The rounds could be misused by any contract killer and the blame would be pinned on the officer and could cost him his job. Poojara was aware that Salaskar's resourcefulness could probably save him from facing the ire of his seniors.

However, even Salaskar drew a blank. But he had a friend he could count on. And thus, he took Poojara to meet Sharma at Mahim. Salaskar knew that whatever Sharma could not troubleshoot with resources, he could solve with unbridled enterprise.

Sharma listened to the story and then seemed engrossed in thought. The gears in his mind began turning. But Sharma did not reveal much and merely asked the two officers to meet him at the end of the day.

Poojara spent the entire day wondering if Sharma could trace the lost ammunition. For all he knew, the bullets could be anywhere in the city. However, Poojara had no option but to pray that Sharma could somehow pull off this miraculous recovery in such a short time. The more he thought about it, the more impossible it seemed. Despite Poojara's scepticism, Salaskar took him along to meet Sharma again in the evening.

'Any luck?' Salaskar asked Sharma.

Sharma opened a packet and laid out the entire missing ammunition on the table. 'Here are Poojara's rounds.'

Poojara couldn't believe his eyes. He picked a bullet between his fingers and held it close to his eye like a jeweller examining a rare diamond. Then, he shifted his gaze to Salaskar and then to Sharma.

'How?' he asked. 'How did you...?'

Sharma was not letting them on to the secrets of his trade. He merely winked and clicked his tongue, as if it was no big deal. He had saved Poojara from a departmental inquiry and a possible suspension at the very beginning of his career. Poojara couldn't stop thanking Sharma, and Salaskar, for their help.

It was widely speculated that instead of tracing the original rounds, Sharma had bought new rounds and given them to the officer who remained shell-shocked when he saw the ammunition. Salaskar too was impressed by Sharma's ingenuity. A few years after the incident, fortune brought them together again and also intertwined their fates in such a way that their lives depended on sticking to each other.

The nineties were the best period for any police officer to make a mark for himself in Mumbai. After escaping from Mumbai and establishing his empire in Dubai, Dawood Ibrahim was spreading his tentacles strongly. It would be prudent for any police officer to snip his growing influence as this would give him fame and clout within the department as well as the masses.

Arun Gawli, who had split from Dawood, was hungry for growth and power. He had thrown a gauntlet at the force. Gawli's attempt at hegemony in central Mumbai had given birth to another ganglord Amar Naik—a vegetable vendor who formed his own gang of desperadoes to stand up to Gawli.

Not only did the police have to put an end to the escalating menace of Gawli, they also had to crush the fledgling might of the Naik gang. Until then, Mumbai Police had always followed the credo of maintaining limited liabilities and not chewing more than they could swallow. Since the 1970s, this *funda* of staying safe and not inviting undue trouble had always haunted the elite force. As a result, petty criminals like David Pardesi and Chandrakant Safalika had the audacity to kill Amirzada and Bada Rajan respectively in the high security precincts of the Mumbai courts in 1983 and 1984.

The mafia was so emboldened at the impotence of the men in uniform that what was unimaginable at one point of time—assaulting the police—became kosher. Dawood's boys had made a desperate bid to avenge his slain brother-in-law, Ibrahim Parkar, by attacking the men involved at J.J. Hospital. When a police team intervened, the assailants did not balk at killing an officer and two constables in September 1992. This was an unprecedented situation where gangsters had no qualms in spraying bullets on the uniformed men on duty.

The city police were going through a precarious period. Morale was at its lowest. In 1992, Salaskar and Sharma, coincidentally or by design, were paired and posted in the crime branch Unit VII in Bandra. Unlike their other batchmates of the class of 83, they had steadily grown in stature and improved their track records since their first posting in 1984. While Salaskar had scored his first encounter in the first year of his maiden posting, it had taken Sharma seven years to get his first hit.

However, both understood the power of the informant network. They realized quite early in their careers that the Mumbai Police with all their sophisticated resources was absolutely useless without the element of a human who whispers authentic information into the ears of a policeman, the ones who provided a valuable tip in the investigation of a major case.

Like most police officers, Sharma and Salaskar pampered their informants, heavily remunerated them for their services and always rushed to their rescue whenever they landed in trouble. The informants also became quite influential in their sphere of activities, garnering affluence. For instance, the man who had called Sharma to report on Javed and Raju outside Pankhe Shah Dargah, rose to become a powerful political activist in the area, ruling the roost in the locality. It is a different story altogether that he still adorns all publicity hoardings with Sharma's photographs on it.

Salaskar too had been extremely helpful and sympathetic to his khabris. He spent long hours with them and treated them like his close confidantes. In fact, Salaskar began paying more attention to his informants than to his own family members. In his quest to excel at his job, Salaskar, who was the eldest among five siblings, began missing festivals and family gatherings. He rarely made it to get-togethers during Diwali or Gudi Padwa, causing much heartburn among his siblings and also his newly wedded wife, Smita.

One of his informants was a drop-dead bombshell, a Pathan beauty, Jaleja. Salaskar knew that while Dawood had escaped, the Pathans were still in Mumbai and their drug syndicate would thrive unabated unless a determined cop intervened. While Salaskar could easily cultivate several informants inside the other mafia groups, it would not be easy for him to find a Trojan horse that could penetrate the ranks and files of the Pathan cartel. But when he struck a rapport with Jaleja and realized that she was willing to be his eyes and ears in the community, Salaskar thanked his stars and began courting her smartly but discreetly. Salaskar's extra attention towards a beautiful and flirtatious woman was misinterpreted by his colleagues in the department. His friend, Sharma, even jokingly told him, '*Ek din yeh apna batwara karegi* (One day she is going to cause a split).'

Salaskar laughed and dismissed it with a wave of his hand. '*Tu bhi ek khoobsurat informant bana le* (You also get yourself a good-looking informant).'

Meanwhile, they had decided to pool their resources together. It was time to take on the Mumbai crime scene.

10

Men of Mettle

Fluorescent pink and neon lights flashed on the sign board of a famous bar in Vikhroli. Ganesh and Subhash Kunchikorve, collectively known as the Makadwala brothers, made their way towards the bar. A durban wearing a red turban recognized the fierce looking men and promptly saluted them. The durban's hand did not drop from his forehead long after Ganesh and Subhash had taken a seat at the table specially reserved for them at the wide entrance. At the bar, a popular Bollywood song thumped aloud: '*Tu shayar hai, main teri shayari*... (You are a poet, and I am your poetry).'

As the city slept, the underbelly of Mumbai's nightlife was just getting started. The bar was teeming with customers but that did not deter Subhash from pulling out the AK-56 rifle he always carried with him. The metallic black weapon glittered under the colourful lights. Subhash sprawled across the cushioned chair with his legs apart and his shoulders stretched wide. In fact, he was using the AK-56 as an armrest! The posture showed his utter arrogance and disdain towards the rule of law and his intentions to shoot at the slightest offence.

Pedestrians passed by the busy street which led to the bar. But they knew that messing with Subhash Kunchikurve meant a certain and painful death. Even local cops did not cross paths with Subhash. He was known to fire even at those who had the gall to look at him in the eye. The waiters at the bar scurried to serve the Makadwala brothers on priority. Their drinks were filled without being asked. Sizzling hot food was delivered straight to their table. And the manager had warned each waiter in advance, 'If you want to live, never ask the Makadwala brothers to pay the bill.'

The term 'Makadwala' referred to the tribe the brothers hailed from. The community was among the fifteen which were declared as criminals in the British era. They lost their right to seek gainful employment and were reduced to the traditional activities of earning a few pennies every day by making trained monkeys (known as makads in the local dialect) dance to their tunes on the street. Other means of livelihood included making brooms and weaving baskets. The community migrated to Mumbai in the early 1930s and settled down in an area which eventually came to be known as the Makadwala Compound in Dharavi.

But Ganesh and Subhash had higher aspirations. They were unwilling to depend on the kindness of strangers to earn their living. In fact, others would beg for their mercy to live. Their tribe had a history of hunting. Good aim and marksmanship came naturally to the duo. And combined with their ruthlessness and their violent antics they soon caught the eye of Anil Parab who was then a lieutenant for Dawood Ibrahim's D-Company. Ganesh and Subhash became the shooters of choice for the Company.

Subhash, who had racked up thirty-six hits against his name, was known to be particularly fond of a Pakistani actress who worked in Bollywood during those days. He exploited the diva to the hilt, making her sing in her nasal voice before making love to her, sometimes by force. The actress never found the courage to file a police complaint. The terror of the Makadwala brothers had shaken the entire city. Unbeknownst to the duo, the dossier of their criminal activities had reached Unit VII of the Mumbai Police Crime Branch. The buddy-pair officers—SIs Vijay Salaskar and Pradeep Sharma—who were as thick as brothers themselves began plotting the downfall of Ganesh and Subhash Kunchikorve.

At the Unit VII office in Bandra, Vijay Salaskar answered a call from Geetika Shastri, his colleague at Mumbai Police who was in awe of Salaskar. Her measured tone indicated that the matter was confidential. Salaskar listened carefully to Geetika as she dictated a vehicle registration number to him. During the entire conversation, Salaskar's face was devoid of emotion. But a plan was already taking shape in his mind. He made a note of the registration number in his diary and disconnected the call. Then he looked across the floor towards his friend and batchmate Pradeep Sharma, who was engrossed in reading the Makadwala brothers' dossier. Each word that Sharma read only strengthened his resolve to bring the criminals to justice.

Salaskar did not make anything obvious. He knew the importance of keeping critical intel under wraps. At this moment, he did not want this news to leak even within the department. So, he patiently kept looking at Sharma until Sharma looked up from the file and met Salaskar's eye. The two cops understood each other well. They were brothers-in-arms in the real sense. One look at Salaskar, and Sharma realized his colleague had something big up his sleeve. Sharma raised his eyebrows twice and asked the golden question in complete silence: what?

Salaskar responded with a slight nod of his head towards the door. *Follow me.* Sharma did not need another invitation. He nonchalantly followed his friend and met him by a tea stall outside. Over a cup of cutting chai, Salaskar told Sharma that he had reliable intel on the Makadwala brothers.

'What do you have?' Sharma asked.

Salaskar told him about the vehicle registration number. 'The car is a blue Maruti 800 belonging to the Makadwala brothers. Recently, it has been sighted frequenting the Vikhroli Parksite area.'

Sharma's eyes lit up. 'Let's get the bastards then.'

'That we will,' Salaskar said.

He was aware that Sharma had worked with the Ghatkopar Police Station, and that Sharma had a solid network of contacts in the area. 'Why don't you probe around Vikhroli? Shake a few informers. See what falls off them.'

The intel on the Makadwala brothers had fallen Salaskar's way through a long sequence of events, the roots of which were established a couple of years ago. In the early nineties, Dawood's hegemony in the underworld was challenged by the gangster Amar Naik who was supported by Krishna Pillai, a strongman of the Vikhroli area. Krishna ensured a steady flow of finance for Naik by building a huge business of bars, *matka* (pot) and bootlegging. He was also engaged in a feud with local politician Lal Singh Chauhan over a nightclub which Krishna Pillai refused to sell. Lal Singh Chauhan also had alleged links with the Company. Dawood knew his dominance depended on cutting off Naik's finances. The mighty don of the D-Company ordered a hit on Krishna Pillai. And he wanted his best shooters—Subhash and Ganesh—on the job.

It did not help Krishna Pillai's case that a certain amount of bad blood had already spilled between him and Subhash. Krishna Pillai was a wealthy, powerful man. Vikhroli was his stronghold. Krishna did not take it lightly that a newcomer like Subhash had dared to establish a footing in Krishna's fiefdom. Social considerations were also at play. Krishna belonged to a higher caste than Subhash. More than once, tempers had flared, and words had been exchanged between the two. Ever since, Subhash was looking for an opportunity to get even with Krishna Pillai.

The Makadwala brothers executed the hit on Krishna Pillai. And Pillai's death changed the life of his son, Kumar, who was then a college student. As the blade of the barber's razor shaved off the last hair from Kumar's head in accordance with Hindu rites, Kumar swore to grow his tresses back only after he had avenged his father's death. He even pledged to walk barefoot until the pyre of Krishna Pillai's enemies burned bright in the cremation grounds of Mumbai.

Kumar savoured his first victory when he eliminated Lal Singh Chauhan outside Borivali train station in the western suburbs of Mumbai. But the Makadwala brothers were still elusive. Kumar, who had taken over the Pillai gang, was hunting them like a man possessed but the shrewd brothers were always a step ahead. By 1993, Kumar was in jail while the Makadwala brothers were alive and kicking on the outside. But only the Makadwala brothers' death could douse the fire of revenge that was burning bright inside Kumar Pillai's heart. He was not the kind who would renege on the promise he had made to his dead father. Being in jail could not be an excuse for failure to fulfil the vow.

Through his lawyer, Kumar conveyed the word to his henchmen that they were to look out for any or all information on the Makadwala brothers. The entire Pillai gang rose to the occasion, some because they genuinely wanted to avenge Krishna's death, and others because they wanted to earn brownie points in Kumar's book. Kumar Pillai's persistence began bearing fruit. Over a period of several weeks, intel was pieced together and conveyed to Pillai through his lawyer.

Kumar bided his time until an officer from the Anti-Narcotics Cell came to visit him in the lock up in February 1993. Some say the officer wanted to interrogate Kumar in an ongoing case. Others say that Kumar had decided to turn informer to get his revenge. And so it was from Kumar Pillai that the police got their first ever piece of credible intelligence about the Makadwala brothers. Kumar told them about the registration number of the blue Maruti 800 which belonged to the Makadwalas and was sighted around the Vikhroli Parksite area.

The same day, the officer shared the intel he had gathered with his colleague Geetika whom he wanted to impress with his clout and informer network. He was blissfully unaware that she, on the other hand, was smitten with Salaskar and his good looks.

Knowing that the brothers' names were on top of the crime branch's list, Geetika called Unit VII and asked for Vijay Salaskar. And thus, the first domino leading towards the elimination of the Makadwala brothers had been tripped.

The next day, early in May 1993, Sharma dressed up in plain clothes and drove an unmarked vehicle to Vikhroli. The summer had brought along searing humidity. Sharma was perspiring down the side of his neck, but that was the least of the policeman's troubles. He turned into the lane leading to the Parksite and found what he was scouring for—a general store which was run by a man he had befriended during his earlier posting at Ghatkopar. Sharma parked his car outside the shop. He leaned on the car to catch the shopkeeper's eye who was busy managing a few customers. Sharma honked twice. The man craned his neck from behind the counter and glanced at Sharma, who was now gesturing to the man to come over. The shopkeeper handed over the business to his staff and rushed towards the car. Sharma asked the man to get inside, which he did. Sharma then moved the car into first gear with his usual ease and began driving around the area. The shopkeeper's face was anxious.

'You have a pen?' Sharma asked.

'Yes sir, at the shop.'

'I didn't drive all the way from Bandra to buy pens from your shop,' Sharma said. He pulled out a white ballpoint pen from his shirt pocket and handed it over. 'Write down this number.'

The shopkeeper had no paper, so he jotted down the number on the flat of his palm. Sharma explained the context of the conversation to his informant and dropped him back to his shop.

'Keep an eye out for the Neptune blue Maruti 800,' Sharma said. 'I'll let you know where to contact me.'

Meanwhile, Vijay Salaskar had conducted a thorough recce of the area. He studied the entry and exit points until he knew them like the back of his hand. He identified three to four spots at safe distances from the lane where he and his colleagues could station themselves. The objective was to be close enough to the lane and thus, to their targets. But Salaskar also had to maintain a fair distance to ensure they did not give their positions away. Salaskar and Sharma decided to man two points personally. The two partners picked positions near commercial establishments with landline phones after convincing the owners to share their numbers for incoming calls. They had barely set up their ambush when Sharma saw something that made him stop in his tracks. He quickly went over to Salaskar and placed a hand on his shoulder.

'Don't turn around,' Sharma said in a low tone. 'But look to your right.'

From the corner of his eye, Salaskar saw a police jeep across the street. Seated at the front was an officer from the Narcotics Cell, and he was accompanied by his team of constables. Salaskar gritted his teeth and looked away.

'*Chutiya!*' Salaskar cussed under his breath. 'Why didn't he bring along a loudspeaker to announce to the world that the Mumbai Police is looking for the Makadwala brothers in this area?'

Sharma could barely contain his laughter at his friend's words. But Salaskar was now hurrying towards the nearest phone. He called senior police inspector Vishnu Kumbhar and told him what he had seen.

'Sir, there is a reason why the Crime Branch is tasked with hunting down dangerous gangsters,' Salaskar said. 'Why is the ANC interfering with our job? What if they scare the targets away? Worse, what if their actions lead to a gun battle in this busy street?'

Kumbhar immediately called the head of the ANC and ordered him to remove his team from the spot immediately. The Crime Branch's encounter specialists were heroes of the day. No one wanted to mess with them. The operation was saved from being sabotaged even before it began.

The Crime Branch started their vigil. Sharma and Salaskar would position themselves every day and look out for the

Makadwala brothers. But after two days of waiting, the Makadwala brothers were nowhere to be found. Sharma and Salaskar discussed the possibility of the information being fake, or perhaps the criminals had got a whiff of their plans. But on the evening of 6 May 1993, the phone in the shop where Sharma was set up rang. Call it a policeman's instinct, but Sharma knew this was *the* call. Indeed, it was the general store manager. His voice was laced with urgency.

'Sir,' the shopkeeper said. 'The blue Maruti with the exact registration number just drove past my store!'

'Which direction exactly?' Sharma asked.

'Amrut Nagar sir,' the shopkeeper said eagerly.

'Are you sure?' Sharma asked. 'Dead sure, sir! I followed them on my bike!'

Sharma almost fell off his seat.

'Are you mad!' he snapped. 'Do you have any idea who is in that vehicle? Get out of there right now!'

Sharma's consternation was well justified. Just the previous year, during Ganeshotsav, the Makadwala brothers were on their way out of a *pandal* (tent) when they saw two men noting down the licence plate number of their car. In full public view, amid the crowd, they stopped their car, stepped out and riddled both the men, who were brothers, full of AK-56 rounds. Then, they coolly stepped back into their car and drove away.

Sharma disconnected the call and furiously punched the numbers on the landline to call Salaskar and the rest of the team. Within minutes, the police party assembled at a pre-decided rendezvous point. Salaskar checked his .38 pistol. It was loaded. Then he asked in chaste Marathi, '*Sahebanna sangitla ka*? (Did you inform the boss?)'

He had just wondered aloud if their superiors had been informed before setting off for the operation as per protocol. Procedure had to be followed. Although a shoot-to-kill was sure to be granted in this instance, they still had to go through the formality.

With each passing second, the possibility of their prey slipping out of their hands was increasing. Police Inspector Shankar Kamble, who was in charge of the Unit, rushed to a nearby public phone and called additional commissioner of police, crime branch, Hassan Gafoor. Within the minute, Gafoor told Kamble to get the Makadwalas 'dead or alive'. He might as well have not bothered with the 'alive' part. Permission granted, Sharma and Salaskar raced towards the police jeep. Kamble caught up with them. Salaskar, who was one step ahead, went around and opened the driver's door. Sharma looked at him quizzically.

'I'll drive, you shoot,' Salaskar said.

Sharma knew his partner was trusting him to not miss and he was determined not to let him down. Sharma nodded and slid into the front passenger seat. He gripped the handle of his 9mm carbine rifle tight. Kamble climbed into the back. Salaskar turned on the engine and the jeep roared to life. The cops were on their way.

The road was dark. No streetlights. Salaskar's hands were firm on the steering wheel. He was excellent at driving in tense situations. The jeep zoomed towards a building. A blue Maruti Suzuki 800 pulled out of the compound and turned towards the main road. The two vehicles were speeding towards each other. Salaskar brought the police jeep to a skidding halt directly in front of the Maruti. He flashed his headlight to check the faces of the occupants inside the vehicle. It was the Makadwala brothers!

The engines of the two vehicles growled like wild animals baying for each other's blood. Salaskar saw the driver of the Maruti move the gear stick. The blue vehicle reversed at high speed and sped away, leaving skid marks in the dirt and black smoke in its trail. Salaskar cursed and pressed his boot on the accelerator. The police jeep took off behind the Maruti 800. The chase was on.

Both vehicles hurtled towards the dark lanes of Parksite, ascending towards the industrial area of Amrut Nagar, at the footsteps of the hillock. The cops had the added responsibility of ensuring that there could not be any collateral damage or pubic loss. But the criminals were not bound by such notions and drove recklessly. A few pedestrians who were walking down the road leaped towards safety. The Maruti jumped over a speed-breaker. The car was light and zipped ahead. Not to be outdone, Salaskar followed suit. The police jeep flew a few good metres in the air and thudded back on the ground. Salaskar had just landed when another car appeared from the opposite direction.

'Watch out!' Sharma shouted.

Salaskar turned the steering just in time. The jeep swerved towards the left, almost tipping over, avoiding a collision only by a whisker. It was a testimony to Salaskar's driving skills that the cops were still in the chase. Sharma, meanwhile, was leaning out of the window and trying to get a shot at the Makadwalas. But the high-speed pursuit and the unpredictable terrain made it nearly impossible. The frenzy of battle took over the cops.

'Shoot through the windshield!' Salaskar yelled.

Sharma was aghast at the idea. He was about to argue when Salaskar finally got close behind the Maruti. In a tactical manoeuvre, he swerved the jeep to the right and matched his speed with the criminal's car. And then, he made the gentlest of contacts with the Maruti. The gangster's car lost control and zigzagged across the road, careening towards a tree. The Maruti crashed head-first into the tree trunk. Black smoke billowed out of the bonnet. In the front seat, Subhash and Ganesh Makadwala were regaining their bearings and turning around in their seats. Subhash squeezed the trigger of his AK-56 just as Salaskar rammed his jeep into the back of the wrecked car. Subhash's aim went haywire. The rat-a-tat of the machine gun flew in all directions.

In the same instant, Sharma, ignoring the jolt of the collision, raised his carbine and fired through the windshield of the jeep into the Maruti 800. A spiderweb of cracks spread all over the windshield. Shards of glass flew in the air. Salaskar and Kamble had already jumped out of the jeep. Salaskar flanked to the right and covered the driver's side. Kamble covered the left. The Makadwala brothers were surrounded. Salaskar began firing his .38. The sound of Sharma's carbine boomed through the air. Bullets pierced through the blue Maruti's metal. Empty cartridges were raining down to the ground. Sharma did not stop until he had emptied the entire clip of his rifle.

Then, suddenly, the gunfire stopped. An uneasy silence descended upon the site. The officers had emptied all their weapons. Sharma pulled out his .38 and made his way towards the criminal's car. Salaskar had already reloaded and provided cover for Sharma.

With the gun still drawn, Sharma saw two bodies on the front seat and one at the back. He opened the door on the driver's side, and Subhash's bullet-ridden body flopped out. In the seat beside him, Ganesh was also dead, his neck twisted in the other direction. The third body in the backseat of the car was later identified as that of Chandrakant Talegaonkar, an associate of the Makadwala brothers. Sharma and Salaskar looked at each other and nodded. They both understood the silent exchange. It was an acknowledgement that each man had held his fort with utmost loyalty. The operation had ended successfully. Subhash and Ganesh Kunchikurve's terror had been eliminated forever.

11

Maniac Mobster Mama

2 February 1993

Sharma had faced lot of hostility in his career but never had there been open sloganeering against him on the open roads except for once. Then, the roads in Andheri east had echoed with the cries of: 'Pradeep Sharma *Murdabad*! Pradeep Sharma Murdabad!'

A crowd of over 10,000 people raising slogans against Sharma were on the road, blocking the traffic. None of them wanted to find out the reason for wishing the cop's death.

However, Sharma could never forget how it all started.

A flight of white birds flew over the high tide at Juhu Beach. The birds chirped aloud in the silence of the morning. A few vehicles passed along the road that led to the beach. John Perreira was walking along the shore with his two-year-old son, William, in his arms. His nine-year-old daughter, Helen, was holding onto his hand. Helen had a school bag strapped on her shoulders, a water bottle dangled from her hand. At this early hour, John was dropping off little Helen to school.

Those days, John felt safe venturing out of his house only during such odd hours. The beach was his home ground. He felt at ease with the churn of the sea. A boat sailed in the distance. John watched the tide and realized this was not the best time for the fishermen to be out there. He was, after all, a fisherman himself who had graduated to a much more lucrative smuggling business later.

'Papa why don't you pick me up from school these days?' little Helen asked.

John wished he could tell her the truth. Instead, he said, 'No, baby. Papa has lot of work all day *na*? How else will Papa buy dolls and chocolates for you and your brother?'

The mention of goodies pacified Helen and she skipped along happily, kicking sand with her boots. William was perched comfortably on John's beefy arm. He snuggled close to his father. John did not let his children sense his fear. A week ago, he had learnt that his *supari* (a contract for his killing) had been floated in the Mumbai underworld.

Smuggling rackets were at their peak. Every beach had its own landing point. And every landing point had its own master. As the rackets grew lucrative, landing agents—mostly fishermen as no one else knew the sea and shore better—started expanding their territories by annexing landing points controlled by their rivals. Men who once worked shoulder to shoulder as fishermen, happily sharing their catch, started fishing for each other's blood.

Robert and Bastya Creado, two brothers from Juhu who also switched from fishing to smuggling, were looking to expand their business. And John's landing points were right next to theirs. When attempts of a peaceful takeover failed, they curried favour with Dawood, who was in India at the time.

Dawood agreed to eliminate John for a price. The job was given to Chhota Rajan, who was then a ground level henchman reporting to Rajan Nair alias Bada Rajan. Chhota Rajan assembled a team of four to five men, which included Anil Parab and Shrikant Desai, and started hunting for their target. John Perreira got wind of the plot to kill him and started laying low. It was only on that morning that he had ventured out of his house.

Unknown to John, Chhota Rajan and his team were watching the beach, suspecting that he might take the scenic route which was familiar to him. Halfway to Helen's school, Rajan and his team had laid their ambush. They were now running towards John with their daggers, swords and guns raised in the air.

John panicked. He spun around and started running. His baby boy in his arms made it impossible for him to gain speed. Each stride felt as if he was running on quicksand. The sounds of his killers rang behind him. He was panting heavily but if he stopped to catch his breath, he wouldn't breathe a second longer. Then he realized something was amiss. Everything had gone quiet. Had his killers given up the chase? He froze when reality dawned upon him. Due to his sheer survival instinct, he hadn't even realized that he had let go of Helen's hand. John stopped in his tracks.

'Papa!' little Helen called out.

Huge waves rose in the Arabian Sea and fell. John Perreira turned around to see one of the assailants kneeling besides his daughter, holding a dagger to her throat.

'I have no wish to kill her,' the man shouted. 'But if you run, I will.'

Trembling and helpless, John walked towards his death with shaky steps. The lamb was trudging towards the butcher. The armed man smiled, admiring the sharpness of the long blade in his hands. Tears glistened in his eyes as John handed over his son to Helen and kissed her forehead. Then, he asked her to run home with her brother as fast as she could. 'No matter what happens,' a tearful John said to his daughter, 'don't look back.'

No sooner had the children vanished out of sight than Rajan and his men stabbed John repeatedly. Blood poured out of John's body and coagulated on the sand. As the final blow ripped apart his intestines, John fell face first into the sand. The rush of a wave frothed around his face. Sea water seeped into his open mouth. John Perreira was dead.

'Now let's get out of here,' Rajan said as he wiped the blood off his face with his shirt sleeve. 'Quickly!'

The hit squad started running towards their cars for a quick escape. However, Shrikant Desai ran towards the sea instead.

'*Ae Mama*!' Rajan called out. 'Are you going for a swim, idiot? Come this way!'

Rajan had used the word 'Mama' as a mild insult. In Hindi and Marathi, making a 'mama' out of someone means making a fool out of them. Desai corrected his course and managed to make a clean getaway. But his fellow criminals refused to let him forget the incident for years. From that day, he was known as Shrikant Mama. Over time, people from Manjrekar Wadi in Andheri where he lived, started calling him Mama, thinking that it was a title given to him out of respect. Mama did nothing to break the illusion.

Residents of Manjrekar Wadi were fiercely loyal to Shrikant Mama, who ruled the entire locality with an iron fist. But he also took good care of his followers. Scores of young men were recruited as shooters for the D-gang because of Mama's influence. They all swore by his name.

Mama first came under the Crime Branch's radar in the early nineties when Sharma and Salaskar were posted with Unit VII in Bandra. Earlier that year, a team of Dawood's shooters, including Naresh Awatu and Sanjay Raggad, barged into a hotel in Lalbaug where Amit Bhogale, one of Ashwin Naik's lieutenants, used to spend his time. They shot Bhogale dead. On their way out, they encountered a police constable. When the constable tried to stop them, they shot him dead as well. As if that were not enough to make the entire police force's blood boil, eyewitnesses told the police after the killers had gunned down the constable, they had also kicked his dead body before leaving. The Mumbai Police top brass decided that enough was enough. It was shoot to kill.

The spate of encounters that followed made several criminals go into hiding. Shrikant Mama, as one of Dawood's chief enforcers and patron saint to many shooters, including Awatu and Raggad, earned a place on the police's hit list.

Sharma and Salaskar picked up all history sheeters from Manjrekar Wadi and grilled them for hours for information on Mama. But the intel they needed came from a completely unexpected source.

Mohan Shedge was a truck driver who also moonlighted as a police informer. On 1 February 1993, he called Sharma and asked if they could meet. Sharma agreed and they met in Bandra. Shedge had a huge smile on his face.

'*Bada tip hai, sir* (I have a big tip, sir),' he said with an air of self-importance. '*Bahot bada!* (It's very big!)'

'*Kiska tip hai?* (About whom?),' Sharma asked.

'I know where Shrikant Mama is.'

Sharma punched the air in utter disbelief. '*Chal bey*! Mama is in Dubai from what I've heard. Are you feeding me rubbish? *Harami*!'

Shedge shook his head vigorously. One of the many pies that Mama had stuck his fingers into were the protection rackets. Mama and his henchmen would collect regular protection money from various classes, which included loaders working in the cargo area at Mumbai airport and truck drivers ferrying goods in and out of Mumbai. Shedge had it from a truck driver that Mama would sit on a chair outside a hotel in Bhilad, Gujarat, and stop all trucks with a Mumbai license plate to demand *hafta* (extortion money) from the drivers in broad daylight.

'Are you serious?' Sharma asked incredulously.

'Have I ever lied to you, boss?' Shedge replied.

'What an idiot!' Sharma said marvelling at Mama's stupidity. But then, he thought, he was called Mama for a reason.

Sharma went back to Unit VII and told Salaskar about the tip off. Salaskar was sceptical too, but Shedge's confidence in his information made both cops load their service revolvers and carbine machine guns. An hour later, they were speeding down the highway to Bhilad. Salaskar was at the wheel. The wind from the open windows blew into Sharma's face. He swayed in the direction of the jeep's turns as Salaskar honked and cut past huge trucks with admirable ease. Sharma's gaze fell on the speedometer which remained constant at three digits. But Salaskar's face was as cool as if he was taking a stroll in the park. The two cops often relied on their confidence of each other's abilities. They were unwilling to let such a big catch get away.

'If this turns out to be a bad tip,' Sharma told Salaskar, 'I'll kill that *harami* Shedge with my own hands.'

The car grinded to a halt outside the hotel Shedge had mentioned. There was a chair outside. And it was empty. Quickly, the two cops barged in and descended upon the hotel manager. In minutes, Sharma scared the truth out of the manager. Mama had indeed been there. But he had left half an hour ago.

'He said he is going home, sir!' the trembling manager told the two cops. 'I swear that's all I know!'

The duo had missed Mama by a whisker. But if they were quick enough, they could still catch him on the way back to the city. If Salaskar's driving on the journey to Bhilad was risky, nothing could have prepared Sharma for the drive back to Mumbai.

'At least you won't have to kill that Shedge of yours,' Salaskar chuckled, glancing towards Sharma.

'*Bhai tu road pe dhyan de* (Brother, you concentrate on the road),' Sharma shot back, clutching the handhold over the passenger's front door.

Salaskar slowed down only when their car snaked into the lanes of Goregaon. Both cops kept their eyes peeled as they drove towards Manjrekar Wadi. This was in February 1993 just after the Babri Masjid demolition. Mumbai was on edge. The government had imposed curfew at night. The streets were totally empty, and as a result Sharma easily spotted Mama near the Royal Challenge Hotel in Goregaon as he was hurrying towards his locality. Salaskar hit the brakes hard. Sharma leaped out of the door even before the jeep had stopped moving.

'Mama!' Sharma shouted. 'Stop!'

Mama spotted Sharma and Salaskar getting out of their car. For a moment, Sharma thought Mama was going to run. Instead, he did something much worse. He whipped out his gun and aimed at the two cops. Sharma pressed the trigger of his carbine. Salaskar followed suit. The whiplash of their guns boomed in the air. Mama's body rattled with the impact of the bullets piercing through his flesh. He was dead before he hit the ground.

Sharma found the nearest telephone booth and called Additional Commissioner of Police Hassan Gafoor to inform him about the encounter. Next, he called the police control room and apprised them of the development. The control room sent a team from the local police station to get the requisite formalities completed.

Both cops left the site in the early hours of the morning. Salaskar dropped Sharma off to his house in J.B. Nagar, Andheri, where he had recently moved in with his wife.

As per the rule, the local police station needed to register a First Information Report (FIR) and Salaskar proceeded to file a report, while Sharma said he would go home. Incidentally, he carried his carbine home, hoping to deposit it the next day at the unit office in Bandra.

An exhausted Sharma showered, letting the water clear his head of the chaos that accompanied the aftermath of an encounter. Then, he went to bed, falling off to sleep instantly.

The next morning, at 10 a.m., the doorbell rang frantically. Sharma's wife Swikriti opened the door and found her neighbour there with a worried look on his face. He told her that her husband had committed a murder and that there was a *morcha* (protest) in front of their building.

Around 700 to 800 people from Manjrekar Wadi had gathered in the building compound, accusing Sharma of 'murdering' their beloved Mama. The horde was baying for Sharma's blood.

Sharma had moved into the house only a few days earlier and had not even installed a telephone yet, which meant he would have to go through the crowd to even find a payphone to call for backup. Shaking his head, Sharma went to the bedroom and picked up the same carbine he had used in Mama's encounter. His wife's protests notwithstanding, he went downstairs and into the lobby.

Sharma knew that only a stunt would work with the crowd.

Before the crowd could react, he raised the machine gun and fired a round in the air. The crowd started running helter-skelter and dispersed within minutes. Sharma then called his office and informed Senior Inspector Shankar Kamble about the incident. A police vehicle was stationed outside the building for the next few days.

Two noteworthy developments followed Mama's encounter. Ravi Pujari, who, at the time, was a D-gang henchman and loyal to Mama, swore revenge against whoever had tipped off the cops about him. He started making inquiries and found out that Sharma had picked up Bala Zalte during his search for Mama. The brothers Bala and Bandya Zalte were the sons of a policeman. They had taken up a life of crime and worked for the D-Company.

Sharma had indeed grilled Zalte for a few hours but he had no idea about Mama's whereabouts, and Sharma had let him off. Pujari thought that Zalte, who had a few cases pending against him, had not been arrested as he had ratted Mama's location to the cops in exchange for his freedom. The same year, Pujari tracked down and killed Zalte.

Meanwhile, Mohan Shedge, who had provided the tip off, dug his own grave. Shedge was a habitual and heavy drinker. The money as well as appreciation he had earned for his tip off became his undoing. '*Mama ko maine marwaaya* (I got Mama killed),' he would boast. '*Abhi mai Mama hoon!* (Now, I'm Mama!)'

More than once, after he was heavily drunk, he claimed credit for Mama's encounter in front of his friends. The news reached Pujari and he soon killed Shedge.

Mama's body, after it was claimed by his family following the post-mortem examination, was placed onto a truck and driven to the Andheri cremation ground. A mob of nearly 10,000 people followed, shouting two slogans against two cops. 'Pradeep Sharma murdabad! Vijay Salaskar murdabad!'

The two friends were happy that they had managed to rid the city of such a villainous man. But one small incident disappointed them.

They had decided to meet Helen to tell her that her father's killer had been served justice by them. They hoped that she, now a college student, would react with some satisfaction and happiness, perhaps even shed tears of joy. However, Helen said she was too young when it had happened and did not recall the incident properly.

Both the friends looked at each other and returned with heavy hearts.

Meanwhile, Mama's partisans wanted to make a chowk in his name to which Sharma complaint to the local DCP and got it removed.

Among the seventy-five criminal cases that the Mumbai Police have registered against Rajan, John Perreira's killing is one that Rajan would face in court.

Sharma had begun to learn the ropes of gangster elimination through the 'encounter method' and was slowly improving on it.

12

Encounter to Entrapment

Sharma's next posting was the in the elite ANC of the Mumbai Crime Branch. The crime branch sleuths usually strutted around like they were hot stuff, superior to the city police. These officers were never assigned routine police duties like patrolling the streets, bandobast, escorting criminals or mohalla policing. They had a clear bailiwick of fighting organized crime in the city.

The crime branch had handpicked officers from the city police and they also boasted of several special niche units within their own close-knit, parallel organization. By way of extension and by virtue of being part of the crime branch, the other specialized units also enjoyed the same privileges and prerogatives as the crime branch officers.

Established in 1989, the ANC was a relatively new unit, and referred to as 'narcotics' within the circles of the Mumbai Police. Now promoted as Assistant Police Inspector (API), Sharma was moved from the crime branch to the ANC on Salaskar's recommendation in May 1993. At ANC, Sharma experienced his next brush with fame, and death too.

In the eighties, the rich and the famous loved their cocaine and heroin. Clandestine rave parties which are now held in pubs and discotheques would earlier be held in the upscale south Mumbai residences. Drug peddling had become common in the by-lanes of the city. Youngsters from affluent families were often found huddled in dark corners of plush localities, passing joints to each other. The menace had even spread to colleges and universities. The authorities were under pressure to provide a befitting response.

Sharma was exposed to a different kind of policing and functioning at the ANC which also involved more ruthless and volatile set of criminals. When Sharma was given independent charge, the ANC had lost its teeth and clout in the city. It was embroiled in controversies when Sharma took over and he realized that the drug peddlers didn't take them seriously; they had no fear of the narcotics officer which made the latter's jobs even more complex and challenging.

Sharma had carefully weighed the benefits of a move to the ANC. Working with a special cell like narcotics meant that he would not be restricted to one area. Since the ANC was part of the crime branch, its jurisdiction extended to the entire city without additional need for clearances or permissions.

Sharma had to work on a two-pronged strategy—to tackle the growing menace of drugs in Mumbai and remove the internal rot in the department. Sharma always believed in unconventional policing methods which is why he was not intimidated by the challenge that lay ahead of him. This fearlessness made him a highly resourceful officer in the department.

Sharma joined the ANC and reported to the erstwhile office carved out in the premises of the Azad Maidan Police Station, which operated from within the precincts of Esplanade Court in south Mumbai. As protocol demanded, Sharma went to call on the commissioner of police, Amarjit Singh Samra. Samra had already heard of Sharma's exploits and was keen to meet him. Sharma briskly entered the cabin, clicked his heels and saluted the police chief. Over a cup of tea, the two officers focussed on using small fish to go after the big sharks.

Known for dishing out platitudes at the unlikeliest moment, Sharma said, '*Sher ka shikaar karne ke liye bakri ki qurbani deni padhti hai* (You need to sacrifice a goat to hunt down a lion).'

Samra merely nodded. The first Sikh police chief in Mumbai, Samra was known to be a no-nonsense cop. During the height of communal riots in the entire country, Samra, who was then head of Thane Police, had managed to keep Thane city totally peaceful because of his leadership abilities. The force looked up to such a competent chief. Sharma had identified the areas where the problem was the worst. But he also had confidence in Sharma's abilities and gave him a free hand in making on-ground operational decisions.

After the meeting, Samra placed his teacup on the desk without a clink. Then he leaned back into his chair, his demeanour calm as always, and outlined a clear mandate for Sharma.

'Clean up the streets, Pradeep,' Samra said. 'Finish the drug mafia! Do whatever it takes.'

Sharma was apprehensive about ruffling too many feathers in the department, but with Samra's green light he was now eager to justify the faith this top cop had placed in him. Sharma resolved to focus on the challenge in front of him—the unabated menace of the drug mafia. Even though narcotics was new territory to him Sharma came up with a strategy to bust the existing drug cartels. He decided to plant a mole who would lead him to the big shark. This was an unprecedented move in the department's history. A specialized agency like the ANC requires different tactics from usual local policing methods. A typical trap would involve the ANC establishing contact with the offender—a drug dealer in this case—through a decoy, known as 'dummy customer'. The dummy would either be a policeman posing as a customer or an informant, or in some cases an informant with some contacts in the drug circuit who could introduce an undercover policeman as his 'friend in need'.

Despite farfetched portrayals in television and movies, laying traps and waiting in plainclothes are the closest an average policeman comes to going undercover. Ask any policeman if they have infiltrated a gang by getting recruited and committing crimes at the behest of a crime lord, and the police will laugh in your face. So, in the Mumbai Police there could be no character or scene like the one Leonardo DiCaprio plays in the film *Departed.* Stuff like that only happens in the movies.

Sharma's first target was a Nigerian drug dealer called Austin Dawson who operated in Bandra. The guy was strongly built and foul mouthed. And Sharma's legwork had finally paid rich dividends in terms of information. He found an informant willing to help him with a trap for Dawson. After careful deliberation, Sharma selected one of his constables, Nitin Vichare, as the decoy. Vichare was a skinny young man who was also a marathon runner. He looked like an underweight bundle of bones rather than a gruff constable. This was a blessing in disguise for Sharma who thought Vichare could easily pass off as a drug addict. Vichare was also keen on winning his boss's approval and was thus ready to go the extra mile. A graduate from Mumbai University, Vichare could speak English better than many officers in the city police. He had failed to crack the officers' exams but was determined to make a mark as a policeman, even if as a constable. The assignment, though fraught with risk, offered him the opportunity to get noticed by the police. Vichare immediately agreed to being Sharma's plant for busting Dawson's drug syndicate.

However, Vichare was also a greenhorn and needed to be prepared for the task at hand. Sharma ensured this with elaborate briefings. 'A trap requires tremendous patience and skill,' Sharma explained to Vichare. 'Display too much eagerness and the drug dealer will smell a rat. This could result in the dealer cutting off all contact. But if you act too hesitant the dealer will lose interest and shoo you away.' He paused. 'In either case, the decoy will be forced to show his hand much earlier than planned. Game over.'

Vichare was quick to grasp the ropes. He was then briefed on the legal aspects. Sharma explained that as policemen, they were bound to work within the boundaries of the law. The downside was that if Dawson was arrested with a small quantity of drugs, it would not amount to much. The Narcotic Drugs and Psychotropic Substances (NDPS) Act—the law which is followed by anti-narcotics agencies in India—specifies clear punitive action against various quantities of drugs. Quantities are classified into either personal (meant for personal consumption of the accused) or commercial (meant for sale to other parties). The definition of these quantities does not depend on the accused's intention. Anyone caught with 'commercial' quantity of drugs is charged with intent to sale, irrespective of whether he wishes to use it all by himself. Similarly, a dealer caught with a small quantity would be charged with intent to use the drugs for personal consumption unless more recoveries are made from him.

The target for Sharma and the ANC, thus, was to catch Dawson in possession of commercial quantities of drugs. Only then could Sharma slap serious charges on the drug peddler and put him away for a long time. If Sharma could get enough cases of commercial quantities against an accused, the court might even consider stronger action against him after his fourth or fifth arrest. However, for a corrupt cop this also meant getting more drugs to sell on the side, making a hefty profit for himself while only charging the drug dealer for a 'personal' quantity possession.

'A drug dealer needs to be wooed before he will meet you with a commercial quantity,' Sharma told Vichare in their final briefing. 'A dealer will move a huge quantity only if he trusts you.'

After a month of preparation, the trap was ready to be laid. Sharma's informant took Nitin Vichare to Carter Road in Bandra where they were supposed to meet Dawson in the evening. On Sharma's instructions, Vichare had worn a t-shirt and jeans and sports shoes to look like a youngster. Vichare and the informant were watching the sun set into the Arabian Sea, waiting for Dawson to arrive. The waves lashed against the shore. Young couples from a nearby college cuddled on the benches. The stench of raw fish emanated from the nearby fishing colonies of Khar Danda. And then, Austin Dawson suddenly showed up. He was wearing a black tank top and blue jeans. The informant introduced Vichare to Dawson as a friend who needed a fix.

'My friend very trustworthy,' the informant told Dawson in broken English. 'He pay well.'

Dawson stared at Vichare's unkempt hair, his fashionable t-shirt and white sport shoes. Vichare's heart was beating so loudly he feared that Dawson would hear it. He calmed himself down. What would happen if Dawson discovered his true identity? The consequences could be fatal. The burly Nigerian moved closer to Vichare. His muscular arms bulged as he flexed his biceps. No wonder the locals were afraid of him. For a moment, Vichare thought Dawson was going to hit him but he only placed his heavy hand on the curve of Vichare's small shoulder.

'I like this man,' Dawson said, laughing, showing off his pearly whites. 'How much do ya want?'

The informer heaved a sigh of relief. Vichare smiled, knowing that Dawson had walked into the trap. Now was the time for caution. Vichare asked for a small amount. This was their first deal. Dawson put his hand deep into the front pocket of his jeans and pulled out a small pouch wrapped in plastic which contained the dangerous white powder, cocaine. Vichare paid Dawson and returned to the ANC head office in Azad Maidan. He handed over the pouch to Sharma.

Sharma patted Vichare's back for a job well done and filed the pouch as evidence. To win the Nigerian's trust, Vichare bought cocaine in increasing quantities over several meetings. Sharma would diligently file each gram of the seized drug. Finally, after a month, Sharma decided to move to the next stage of the trap. Vichare told Dawson that he needed a bigger quantity of the powder for a party next week. After some haggling and discussion, a deal was fixed for one kilogram of cocaine. For a drug that is sold in grams, one kilogram was a big quantity.

The D-day arrived. The deal was scheduled in a small lane near Mehboob Studio, which is located at the corner of a huge merry go round road. Five roads lead to different directions. At any point of time, it is busy intersection and pedestrians find it difficult to cross the circle. The police team had the arduous task of not only being on watch on a such complex road but also to ensure that their operation did not end in disaster after all their hard work.

Sharma arrived an hour before the specified time in a private car and waited, posing as a young man waiting for a friend. Some in his team arrived before him, others after him. Some took their assigned positions at the mouth of the lane, some farther away. Sharma had meticulously planned the deployment in advance. The policemen had now blocked all exit routes.

Dawson arrived at the designated lane. His physical presence made him stand out in the crowd. Sharma had an imposing personality himself, but he also had the ability to blend into a crowd when he wanted to. He was nearly invisible in the sea of pedestrians, and yet he was watching Dawson like a hawk. Five minutes later, Vichare walked into the street. Sharma had given him strict orders to not look in his direction. Vichare followed the order to the T and walked straight up to the dealer.

'You got ma money, man?' Dawson asked in his accented English.

Vichare nodded and showed him the bag he was carrying.

Dawson extended his beefy hand. 'Give me the fucking money.'

'What about my stuff?' Vichare asked, hesitating. He had to let the dealer think that he had the upper hand but at the same time could not blow the deal.

'I have your stuff. But money first.'

Vichare handed over the bag. Dawson unzipped the bag and peered inside. He reached inside with one hand and made sure all the paper he felt was indeed currency. Then he looked up and smiled. Before Vichare could realize what was happening,

Dawson pushed him to the ground and started running away with the bag. Vichare screamed in Sharma's direction.

'Sir, he is running away!'

Sharma was not only alerted but showed amazing alacrity as he jumped out of his car and ran towards the dealer, gun drawn.

Dawson was faster. He sped towards the Mount Mary slope. Though Sharma was in good physical condition he was no match to the Nigerian's moves. Dawson's long legs had given him a substantial lead over the cops. If he vanished today, Sharma thought, Dawson would never be found. To top it all, Dawson had a bagful of the department's money. The entire operation would turn out to be a disaster. Sharma would not only lose face in front of the police chief, but they would end up becoming the laughing stock of the Mumbai Police.

Sharma ran fast and hard but Dawson still increased the distance between them. Suddenly, Sharma noticed that another policeman was closing in on Dawson. It was Nitin Vichare, the marathon runner!

Dawson too noticed Vichare catching up and realized that he would never be able to outrun Vichare. He stopped in his tracks and turned. For a moment, Vichare thought Dawson was about to surrender. But Dawson stuck a hand into the back of his jeans and pulled out a gun. The gun was now aimed at Vichare, who immediately halted the chase, trying to keep his distance from Dawson by backing away. Behind him, Vichare heard the approaching sounds of Sharma's boots.

Dawson was sweating from head to toe. His eyes had turned red with rage. Out of breath, Sharma realized that Dawson would kill Vichare to punish him for setting up the trap. Just as Dawson opened fire at Vichare, he ducked and saved himself. When Sharma shot at Dawson, he moved aside, realizing that it was Sharma who had the gun, not Vichare. He had to get rid of Sharma first. Dawson turned towards Sharma and was ready to shoot.

Sharma knelt on the ground and squeezed off three rounds one after the other. His bullets, which were aimed at the leg and thigh area, hit Dawson in the lower abdomen. Dawson fell to the ground. Then Sharma kept his weapon pointed towards Dawson's fallen body fearing a round of firing from him while on the ground. When Dawson did not fire, Sharma approached him with utmost caution to make sure that the threat had been neutralized.

Yes, Dawson was dead.

Traffic came to a screeching halt at the Mehboob Studio junction. The police control room informed the Bandra police about the firing. The sound of approaching police sirens rang through the air.

This was September 1993, only a few months after the serial bomb blasts in March. The city had barely recovered from the trauma of the biggest terrorist attack on India. A firing incident on a busy lane in the plush Bandra area would come under the media scanner. But Sharma had to save his man at the cost of a gangster's life. He would stand by his decision if it was questioned. Police jeeps, vans and other patrolling cops converged on the spot. Crime branch officers from Unit VII too made a beeline for the spot. In the meantime, Sharma had called and briefed his immediate superiors about the incident so that Commissioner of Police, Amarjit Singh Samra, could be made aware of the development.

Once again, Sharma was hailed as a hero because he had rid Bandra of a very notorious drug peddler. However, Sharma knew that Vichare was the operation's real hero. Had it not been for Vichare's patience, resilience and willingness to risk his life, the ANC squad would have never got the scalp of such a big drug dealer. The department threw its might behind Vichare by helping him with the resources needed to crack the PSI's exams. Motivated by the support of his superiors, Vichare diligently prepared for the exam. This time, he cracked the exam and he was absorbed into the force as SI Nitin Vichare.

And Pradeep Sharma went on to learn the new skills in policing—from encounters to entrapments.

13

Bombay's Breaking Bad

It was an incredible sight.

Nothing a seasoned cop would be prepared to witness in all its length and breadth. Sharma could not believe what he was seeing. By now, Sharma had spent over a decade in the police department, of which six months were in the ANC, so this was not only unexpected but totally baffling.

Once Sharma got over his astonishment, he turned to look at his men who had followed him to the room after him. Their faces wore a look of bewilderment and consternation. Sharma had come to Kurla to gather evidence against a reputed medical doctor in the area. But Sharma never anticipated that he would be faced with this unbelievable mountain of evidence staring at him in Imtiyaz's bedroom.

Not even a year had passed since the serial blasts of March 1993 that had rocked the city. The blasts, coming on the heels of the Babri Masjid demolition and two bouts of violent communal riots, had torn to shreds the city's cosmopolitan fabric. Sharma's seniors had been reluctant to grant him permission to raid a predominantly Muslim locality in Kurla. But past records of success and impeccable credentials forced the crime branch bosses to let Sharma have his way.

The north eastern suburb of Kurla is known for two things—cheap real estate and abjectly dirty and unhygienic surroundings in a cluster of predominantly Muslim localities. In fact, a major segment of Kurla Pipe Road is referred to as Mini Pakistan due to the heavy presence of Muslims in the locality.

Kapadia Nagar was constructed on the C.S.T Road in Kurla with several blocks of buildings comprising over 752 flats in the late eighties. Back then, it was regarded as a posh locality in Kurla area. Muslims took pride in buying properties in the colony. The plush Bandra Kurla Complex (BKC) spread over 730 acres of land, which suddenly sprang up behind the colony, was yet to be conceived.

The colony had a prominent masjid outside. Green flags with crescent and stars fluttered everywhere and asserted the presence of a Muslim stronghold. Sharma and his men had entered the colony to the overtly hostile gaze of curious onlookers. But Sharma was not a part of a mohalla policing brigade. He was in no mood for wooing the Muslim community elders or youths.

Sharma's intel suggested that Dr Imtiyaz Shaikh, MBBS, a reputed doctor in the area, was a top drug dealer in the city and a close associate of India's biggest drug baron Iqbal Memon alias Iqbal Mirchi—the greengrocer turned India's most notorious, globe-trotting, fugitive drug lord. Sharma wanted to dismiss the tip off as false. What if it was a motivated plant, engineered with the agenda of using the police machinery to malign a good Samaritan?

Dr Imtiyaz Shaikh was known to be a low profile, philanthropist doctor, who dispensed free medicines to the needy. Endless rows of patients would throng his clinic. But Sharma's source was one of his most reliable informants, Omprakash Singh alias OP, who was posted as inspector of quality control at the Mazgaon docks. OP's tips had never failed Sharma in the last three years. He came from a family of academicians in Ghatkopar. His father was a professor of Hindi at Ramniranjan Jhunjhunwala College in Ghatkopar and his elder brother, Arun Singh, was a professor of Science. OP was studying to follow in their footsteps when fate suddenly stuck a dagger in the heart of all his ambitions.

In 1991, a D-gang member named Lalsingh Chauhan was shot at in Ghatkopar by Ashwin Naik's gang men. The firing incident happened right outside the building where the Singh family lived. And from the window of his first-floor apartment, Arun witnessed the entire murder.

Sharma was posted with the Ghatkopar police at the time and he met Arun during his inquiries. Arun agreed to become a witness in the case and identify the shooters in court.

Unfortunately for OP, Naik learned about his intentions. Many cases registered in the nineties have fallen through simply because no witness dared to corroborate the prosecution charges. Gangsters paid heavy sums of money to their moles in the police force to find out who was appearing as a witness against their henchmen. The witness would then be mercilessly eliminated. When Arun decided to depose, he met the same fate. Naik told Kumar Pillai, his top aide, to track down Arun and kill him. Arun was shot down outside Ram Niranjan Jhunjhunwala college near Ghatkopar west train station in broad daylight.

Arun's death was a blow not only to the case against Naik but also to OP, who swore that he would not rest till he had extracted his revenge. Since an average Indian learns about crime and criminals from Bollywood, OP too took a leaf out of the movies. Zeenat Aman's character in the blockbuster *Don* seemed to be the right way forward for him. In the movie, the actress joins a gang and begins squealing to a senior police officer. So, OP got in touch with Chhota Rajan and swore allegiance to him. At the same time, since he also knew Sharma through his brother, OP tracked him down to the Narcotics Cell and revived contact.

OP also kept in touch with other police officers he knew to conduct a two-pronged assault on the Naik gang. OP's job at the Mumbai Port Docks provided a good cover and was useful because it brought in massive amount of information without him even chasing it.

On the other hand, Sharma was seething since the Austin Dawson encounter at Bandra in September. Sharma had won the gratitude of Bandra residents by eliminating a notorious drug peddler, but he was totally mystified when the press and news channels began calling him a trigger-happy cop. The human rights activists dubbed the Austin Dawson encounter to be an extra judicial killing. Instead of appreciating the bust-up of a major Nigerian cartel and cutting off a critical drug supply to the suburbs, Sharma was burdened with an avalanche of hostility.

Media reports claimed that Sharma was no Sherlock Holmes, he was only Dirty Harry (a trigger-happy character made famous by actor Clint Eastwood in a 1971 movie of the same name). Sharma decided to pick up the gauntlet and prove everyone wrong. He holstered his gun and wore an investigator's hat for the philanthropist doctor's case.

Police work is based on collecting negligible information and processing trivial clues. A lot of legwork is employed while chasing cold calls. Several dots are connected to form a larger story. Only then does a clear picture in any investigation emerge.

It needs relentless patience, consistent follow up and clinical precision to convert a link into successful detection.

However, a link, like a trap, is a crucial technique in the art of investigation. It means picking up smaller fry and squeezing him for information for the man above him. The process is repeated with every link in the chain till the police can net the biggest fish in the ocean.

In January 1994, the memories of Dawson's killing were still fresh in public memory. Human rights activists were calling it murder. The court had come down heavily on the ANC. Sharma desperately needed a win.

But after the serial blasts in Mumbai, the Muslim population in the city came under the scanner of the authorities. Any Muslim with the slightest connection to the smallest crime was picked up. The Special Investigating Team set up by Police Commissioner A.S. Samra, under the leadership of then DCP Rakesh Maria, had picked up thousands of suspects and interrogated them for hours together for one measly piece of information. It was by following these links that the Team could crack the entire case within days. The same was true for other units as well.

Humint (as CIA sleuths call human intelligence), or khabris in the lingo of the Mumbai Police, had totally dried up for them as most of their informants were Muslims. Crime branch units were reeling under the acute crunch of intelligence on the underworld and their activities.

Sharma was desperately looking to solve a big case to prove the media wrong. Planting a mole like Vichare in a drug lord's network was no mean feat, and yet Sharma was not lauded enough for it. And OP was exactly the trojan Sharma was looking for.

OP swore upon everything holy that the good doctor was selling brown sugar.

Sharma found it hard to believe but decided to place Dr Shaikh under surveillance. For weeks, Sharma's team kept a discreet watch on the doctor as well as the clinic. Their surveillance revealed that the man was no ordinary person. Every morning, the doctor would go to his clinic and attend to patients till night, after which he would shut shop. However, instead of going back to his house in Kapadia Nagar, he would take a detour to another flat where he would spend a couple of hours before finally going home.

Sharma's initial thought was that the doctor was having an affair, and that OP was wasting his time. If not a mistress, perhaps Imtiyaz had a second wife secretly tucked away. But the surveillance team also observed that every few days, shady looking characters—every cop develops a radar for them after a couple of years on the job—would visit him at home. These visitors would always be armed with carry bags and would walk very quickly, whether towards Imtiyaz house or away from it. Veteran constables from the ANC were asked to assist with the surveillance and lend their expertise. Most of them agreed that Imtiyaz's visitors were thin to the point of emaciation. Malnourished men usually meant drug addicts.

On a sunny afternoon, a team of ANC officials led by Sharma descended on Dr Imtiyaz Shaikh's house in Kapadia Nagar. The running theory was that he was purchasing drugs from wholesalers and selling them from this house. Their theory was shot to bits the minute the ANC entered the doctor's secret house. Inside the bedroom was a fully equipped laboratory, complete with various chemicals used for synthesizing brown sugar and other narcotics. Various pipes were connected to volumetric flasks. Huge quantities of a granular, white substance was stashed at the side. A chemistry student himself, Sharma immediately understood this was a drug processing unit.

Dr Imtiyaz Shaikh wasn't just selling drugs, he was making them. To apply a modern analogy, Dr Imtiyaz wasn't a Jesse Pinkman, he was a Walter White. White and Pinkman are pivotal characters in the hugely popular *Breaking Bad* series on Netflix. Pinkman is a drug supplier and White a reputed science professor who creates top quality stuff. The series that came at least two decades after Dr Imtiyaz was busted is a testament that reality preceded fiction and was much stranger.

The stunned ANC officers called the Central Forensic Sciences Laboratory (CFSL) in Kalina and requested a team to be sent to them immediately. Imtiyaz was arrested at his clinic and taken to the ANC headquarters. The same evening, the head of the CFSL team gave an unofficial verbal confirmation to Sharma that the set up inside Imtiyaz's house was a full-fledged drug lab. He promised to send the official reports as soon as possible.

It made sense, Sharma thought. Being a doctor, Imtiyaz had the knowledge as well as the wherewithal for the job. He brought ingredients from various small to medium suppliers who didn't care what their products were being used for as long as the money was good. If anyone asked, Imtiyaz had the perfect answer: 'for research purposes'. He would then process the ingredients to create the drugs and sell them to low level suppliers not in grams but in kilograms, and thus make a killing.

Imtiyaz's arrest, although a big catch, was only the first link in the chain. Cracking the doctor was no easy task. He was different from the average street peddler that the ANC usually arrested and was unwilling to cooperate with the police. Sharma decided to put his interrogation skills to use with a subtle mix of psychology and his own interrogation techniques.

One night, Imtiyaz was having dinner in the ANC lock up. Sharma entered the room for an 'informal' chat. Sharma told Imtiyaz that it pained him to interrogate a doctor. The doctor was curious to know the reason behind this sympathy. Sharma revealed that he came from a family of 'doctors' and did not want to use torture against someone from a profession he deeply respected. And by next morning, Imtiyaz was singing like a canary. But Sharma had conveniently omitted one crucial detail: his father and elder brothers had the title of doctor because they were PhD holders! He had applied a variation of the Stockholm Syndrome without Imtiyaz realizing it.

Through the interrogation, Sharma identified a whole range of drug dealers in the central and eastern suburbs and initiated a massive crackdown. Over a dozen vital conduits in the trade were picked up and thrown behind the bars. But the most important 'link' Imtiyaz gave Sharma was Nitin Patel, a close associate of drug lord Iqbal Mirchi.

Iqbal Memon alias Iqbal Mirchi, a Mumbai native who died of a heart attack in London in 2013, was India's biggest drug dealer. The Indian government had failed to extradite him from London despite spending crores of rupees in a long-drawn legal battle at Bow Street Court. Instead, the government had to shell out a hefty sum in damages. Mirchi's other claim to fame was being married to starlet Heena Kausar, the daughter of filmmaker K. Asif, who made the historical *Mughal-e-Azam*. Heena also played a cameo in the film.

The ANC picked up Nitin Patel for interrogation. Not wanting to spend too much time hung upside down in jail, Patel quickly bought his freedom by putting Sharma onto the

Bhanushali brothers, Nitin and Nayan. '*Kya hai maloom nahi, sir, lekin jo bhi hai bada haath maar rahe hain. Maa kasam bol raha hoon!* (I don't know, sir, but they are going in for the big kill, I swear on my mother),' the drug dealer assured the cops.

A dragnet was spread for the Bhanushali brothers. Several days of pursuing one link after another, Nayan and Nitin were finally picked up. Of course, they professed innocence and threatened to rain legal hell on the ANC for harassing them. But a search of their house revealed documents issued by the customs department which had just cleared a consignment of the brothers to be sent to Maputo in South Africa. With Patel's claims about *something big* still fresh in his head, Sharma raced to the customs office at Indira docks and traced the clearing house agent (CHA) who had issued the clearance.

The CHA said that the Bhanushali brothers had obtained clearance to export red oxide (*geru*) to Maputo. Sharma demanded to inspect the consignment over the protests of the CHA which had already inspected and sealed the container. True to Sharma's hunch, the cartons inside the container had packets of red oxide in the front and tablets of mandrax in the back. The consignment was caught just two days before it was scheduled to be shipped to Maputo.

They had seized 5000 kgs of Mandrax tablets—the largest haul made by a single cop in a single case anywhere in the world. This was Sharma's big achievement in the first decade of his service.

Sharma, who had decided to use only his wits and not his weapon to solve the case, had earned a gratifying victory. Sharma's seniors showered accolades on him, and the media went gaga over his achievements. Finally, Sharma was at peace with himself.

But while Sharma was chasing the Bhanushali brothers, Dr Shaikh was secretly plotting his freedom. After spending fourteen days in police custody, Imtiyaz was sent to judicial custody. Then, he filed an application in Bombay High Court seeking parole on the grounds that his mother had passed away, and he needed to complete her last rites in Panvel.

The court immediately sanctioned his instant parole. It was later explained that the judge had ruled on humanitarian grounds.

Imtiyaz jumped parole the same day and never returned. When he failed to report to Kurla Police Station on the third day of his parole as per the terms, the police sent a report of the same to the ANC. The court which had granted bail then issued a sternly worded order to the ANC to track him down and threw in a few lines about police laxity for good measure while Sharma stood silently grinding his teeth.

Despite Sharma's best efforts to trace him, Imtiyaz is still absconding. Inquiries at the time indicated that he fled to South Africa. There was also a tip off about him being in Bangalore in 2018, which never panned out. Dr Imtiyaz, the desi Walter White, has now been on the wanted list for twenty-four years. The Mumbai Police and Interpol are still looking for him.

14

Friends Turn Foes

'No, Vijay, I cannot let him go. The evidence against him is compelling,' Sharma was arguing with Salaskar who was getting increasingly irritated with his explanation.

'This is a matter of life and death for my informer,' Salaskar was trying hard to persuade his friend of ten years and his best buddy in the department.

'And this is about my prestige. What is dearer to you? My prestige or the risk to your informer's life?' Sharma tried to articulate his insecurities in the best possible manner.

Salaskar kept staring at Sharma for a long time, then rose in a huff, pushed the chair behind and walked out of the door quietly without saying a word.

The biggest friendship in the police department that was ever formed had broken over a minor disagreement.

The two friends, who had survived bigger storms together, parted ways because of an ordinary argument.

The seeds of discord had begun to germinate immediately after they were separated from Unit VII of the crime branch and Sharma was shifted to the ANC soon after the Makadwala encounter in 1993 end. They had lost touch and become engrossed in their own individual successes and investigations. Rarely would they interact or find the time to meet each other like in the earlier days. As the famous maxim goes, you are as good as your last detection, and neither of them wanted to lose out. Refusing to rest on their past laurels, they were always constantly striving to improve their career track record.

Salaskar who had earlier served a stint in narcotics cell had wholeheartedly dedicated himself to his work at the ANC. Since Salaskar was keen on making a name for himself even in the narcotics department, he pulled all stops.

Despite scores of other informants, Salaskar's most trusted informant was the Pathan beauty Jaleja who also turned out to be very useful for him during the course of investigations. Since Jaleja and her machinations have been profiled at length in *Byculla to Bangkok*, we will skip her background here.

Jaleja knew how to manipulate the drug peddlers and snare them to the point of destruction. Mumbai's biggest drug peddler, Nari Khan, was her most infamous victim. The drug lord who once was easily estimated to be worth over Rs 400 crore died a pauper's death, his body lying unclaimed for over ten days in the J.J. Hospital morgue. No Pathan organization or family was willing to associate themselves with Khan even through the funeral rights. Such was the venom of her affiliation with drug lords.

Salaskar liked the way she could ferret out information from the deepest cavities of the Pathan cartel. He had begun to rely on her after a couple of successful narcotics case investigations in which she had been a vital conduit.

In the police circles, the value of an informant is directly proportional to the number of breakthroughs he or she will provide

Arbaaz Khan, accompanied by Shera, reaching and exiting the Thane Anti Extortion Cell (AEC) for questioning in connection with the Sonu Jalan case.

Sonu Jalan being taken out of Sharma's cabin to the AEC lock up.

Police Inspector Rajkumar Kothmire, Thane AEC, displays a 'line machine' that allowed bookies to connect to multiple parties at the same time to accept bets.

Sharma leading Iqbal Kaskar out of Haseena Parkar's Dongri residence on the night of his arrest.

Iqbal Kaskar in police custody following his arrest.

Iqbal Kaskar

Sharma being felicitated by Mumbai Police Commissioner M.N. Singh after he eliminated Rafiq Dabbawala, a member of the Subhash Singh Thakur gang, who had 170 cases registered against him and was on the top ten most wanted list. Also seen in the picture is Joint Commissioner of Police (Crime) Bhujangrao Mohite.

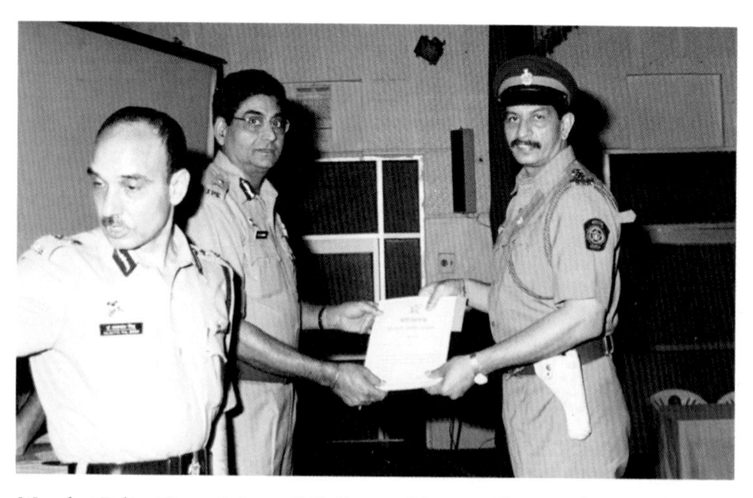

Mumbai Police Commissioner R.S. Sharma felicitates Sharma after the encounter of the LeT operatives in Mumbai. Also seen in the picture is Joint Commissioner of Police (Crime) Satyapal Singh.

Mumbai Police Commissioner Ronnie Mendonca felicitates Sharma at the Naigaon police grounds after the encounter and arrest of the accused who helped gangster Firoz Kokani escape from police custody. A constable was shot dead during the escape.

A very young Sharma posted at the Ghatkopar Police Station, seen with his team that solved a string of dacoity cases in Ghatkopar.

Pradeep Sharma

Pradeep Sharma with
his wife Swikriti.

Sharma with his wife, daughters and father receiving the Rajiv Gandhi Award for his contribution to society through his service as a police officer in Mumbai in 2004. Sharma is the only officer to receive this award in the country.

in major investigations. Jaleja, being a Pathan girl, was invariably involved in almost all the cases related to the drug syndicate run by the Pathans and busted by Salaskar. Thus, Salaskar became quite protective of her and did not want to lose her.

However, a major controversy erupted in the narcotics cell. Allegations surfaced that the top rung officers were involved in selling off the seized narcotics in the market instead of disposing them. Some of the senior officers were alleged to have a serious nexus with the drug peddlers and instead of arresting them under the stringent NDPS Act, they had started conniving with them for pecuniary gains. The collusion and connivance of the cops with the drug peddlers which was a secret until then was exposed. The whole department was in shambles, with the reputation of the officers in tatters.

The crime branch bosses, who until then were in total denial, faced major embarrassment from the central agencies of the Narcotics Control Bureau (NCB) when they were confronted by the top brass with the clinching evidence. The *Indian Express* published transcripts of the conversation between the police officers and the drug lords on their front page, discussing the dismissal of case and the commercial compensation.[2]

Consequently, to ensure a total cleansing of the department and to save face, the entire narcotics cell was summarily shunted out and the officers were replaced at every level. Salaskar, who was steadily ascending in the department, found that he had become collateral damage when he too was transferred along with tainted officers.

---

[2] S. Hussain Zaidi, 'How a Police Officer Helped Notorious Druglord Fool the Law', *Mumbai Newsline*, *Indian Express*, 6 December 1996.

Salaskar could not believe his bad luck.

Salaskar was then posted in crime branch Unit VII in Bandra office along with Sharma where they both formed an A Team and scored several enviable encounters including the Makadwala brothers and Srikant Mama—all top aides of Dawood Ibrahim.

In 1993, Sharma was moved to the narcotics cell and incidentally was given charge of the post which Salaskar had held earlier. The problem between the friends started after this administrative transfer.

Initially, Salaskar was relieved to know that his best friend Pradeep Sharma was posted in the narcotics cell. He was reassured that Sharma could carry forward his investigations and both could share the plaudits. Salaskar also anticipated that Sharma would provide the same amount of amnesty and long rope to his informants that he extended while he was posted at the narcotics cell. However, he was soon disappointed at the turn of events.

Sharma was unaware of Salaskar's grand plans. He was posted in narcotics cell at a time when the reputation of several celebrated officers had been tainted. Restoring the department's old pride was an important mission for the new crop of officers. Sharma did not want to make the smallest mistake.

Sharma's string of successes at the ANC had come at a heavy price. Those who were newly shifted to the cell were paranoid about their own survival in the department and were acutely aware of departmental surveillance on them.

Soon after Sharma took over, he had launched a massive crackdown on all active drug peddlers and conduits in Mumbai. His network of informants, cultivated and nurtured over the years, was regarded as the best in the city. Among the Pathans, he had tamed Sarmast Khan who provided Sharma with all the essential intelligence. Naturally Sharma picked up history sheeters, squeezing them to the core. He went after known addicts in the lower strata of society, gleaning information about retail and wholesale suppliers.

Sharma's indiscriminate rounding up inadvertently included some men who were informants for his friend Vijay Salaskar. When these informants began to face the heat from Sharma, they realized that they were not going to enjoy the same immunity they had received from Salaskar who was far more flexible and forgiving. Subsequently, they made a beeline to Salaskar's office in Nagpada, and he, in turn, felt that he could influence Sharma.

Salaskar tried to intervene on behalf of his men but he realized that it was not going to be as smooth as he had expected. Sharma endeavoured to keep Salaskar happy, but he had his limitations. At times, Sharma failed to help Salaskar and he presumed that Salaskar would understand his point in time. However, Salaskar got increasingly miffed with Sharma and misconstrued it as his arrogance and highhanded methods.

The flashpoint came when Salaskar wanted Sharma to go slow on Jaleja's boyfriend, Khalid Usman. Sharma initially obliged his friend and even went beyond his own expectations. Sharma implicitly followed Salaskar's intelligence, also helping Salaskar in the encounter of Jaleja's stalker, Gul Jaman Khan. But later, Sharma felt that something was amiss. Things did not add up. Sharma, who had been quite particular in heeding to Salaskar's requests realized, that they were becoming too frequent and unbearable.

Sharma decided that he would try to make Salaskar understand that his intervention for Salaskar's informants could not become a regular routine. He began keeping count of Salaskar's requests.

'This is the fourth time in a week that you have called with a similar request,' Sharma replied, irritated with his friend.

He decided to put a stop to such requests and told Salaskar that he could not grant amnesty to his people anymore. Sharma knew that Salaskar would be upset with him, but he thought that his old friend would understand and come around.

Salaskar interpreted Sharma's refusal as a lack of personal loyalty and insolence because of his rising popularity in the department. Sharma was riding high after successfully bringing down Bandra's notorious drug supplier, Dawson. Salaskar thought this has gone to his head.

While Sharma was struggling with his own demons. The media carried out a campaign against him and a few seniors were not too happy with the way he had killed Austin Dawson.

One day, Salaskar barged into Sharma's cabin in at Azad Maidan and reminded Sharma that he should not become arrogant with his success. Sharma was stunned at Salaskar's reactions. He could not believe that Salaskar was upset with him over informants who were, after all, dispensable.

These events marked the beginning of a cold war between the two young, hot-blooded cops. A great friendship had disintegrated because of a small misunderstanding, and soon it escalated to a professional contest, snowballing into a full-blown rivalry. What the underworld and the mafia could not manage to achieve, the two friends inflicted upon themselves voluntarily and this pleased the mafia.

The rivalry evolved in such a way that there was a vertical split in the police department. It seemed that an invisible line had been drawn. One could either support Sharma or Salaskar, and they could not be friends with both. The department colleagues, their bosses in the top brass, bureaucrats, political activists, journalists, corporate houses and non-governmental organizations (NGOs) all chose their favourite among the two.

Sharma and Salaskar too made their choices clear. They would not follow the path of others. They would blaze their own trail. If Sharma decided to decimate the city's biggest gang, the Dawood Ibrahim syndicate, managed by his top lieutenant, Chhota Shakeel, then Salaskar decided to concentrate on Mumbai's most powerful oligarchy of the Arun Gawli gang. Salaskar felt that by virtue of being local, the latter gang could undermine the law and order in a much more damaging manner. In 1995, there was a shift in power in the state from Congress to the Shiv Sena. And this provided an impetus to Salaskar's aspirations.

These decisions might look like a fallout of professional competitiveness, but the police bosses were delighted with the results because it would have only meant elimination of the foot soldiers who slavishly followed the diktats of their bosses hidden in foreign shores. The concerted crackdown of Sharma and Salaskar would clearly serve as deterrent for further recruitment of sharpshooters thus upsetting the apple cart.

But the rivalry also had a flip side to it. While Salaskar felt that to become powerful one should align themselves with the powers that be, Sharma had a totally different philosophy.

'You never know if the existing powers are willing to collaborate with you. So why devalue your importance by making a punt and getting rebuffed. Rather create your own power. This way you own the power and not vice versa,' he is known to have said.

The naked ambitions of these two erstwhile friends and heroic cops and their dangerously selfish principles had far reaching ramifications for the city police.

15

Chandan Chowky

As he made his way up to the first-floor office of DCP Satyapal Singh, Zone VII, Sharma could not stifle a chuckle. Walking a step ahead, Senior Police Inspector Firoze Ganjia half-turned around and shot Sharma a quizzical look while climbing the stairs. He wasn't interested in what Sharma found funny. He just wanted the man gone. Had he asked, Sharma would have had a funny story to tell. In 1996, he had found himself locking horns with the same man he was going to meet right now.

Sharma had his first brush with Singh just after the encounter of a Nigerian drug dealer near Regency Hotel in 1996. Given the equation between the two men today, one wouldn't believe that their relationship began with discord. Sharma, who was with the ANC at the time, found out within days of the encounter that Singh, as the DCP in charge of the zone, was trying to put together a 'negative report' about the encounter.

In police parlance, a 'negative report' is a report submitted by a superior and competent authority that certifies that the encounter had been staged. This makes the officer who conducted the encounter liable to face inquiry and possibly be arrested and tried as a murder accused, a fate that Sharma would one day have to face. And that too from a DCP sitting in the same office.

A very disturbed Sharma had approached DCP Hemant Karkare, who was heading the ANC at the time, and told him what he had heard. He had, since the first day, always operated on Karkare's orders and his vision to clean up the city of the drug menace as well as the ANC of the controversies surrounding it.

What Sharma did not know was that Karkare, too, was operating on the direct orders of the then Police Commissioner R.D. Tyagi. A no-nonsense officer feared by everyone working under him, Tyagi didn't exactly ignore the rules but believed that they were meant to create convenience, not inconvenience. He had no patience for officers who refused to see the larger picture and those who chose to hide behind the comfort of rules instead of showing a little initiative which would harm no one.

Karkare made his own inquiries and after confirming that Singh was indeed preparing such a report, quickly called Tyagi. The top cop, after listening patiently to Karkare, shook his head and called Singh. Mincing no words, he told Singh that if he was incapable of doing good work himself, he should at least not try to meddle with other people's efforts.

The same Singh, a year later, constituted his own special squad to protect the rich and famous in his area—which stretched from Andheri to Bandra—who found themselves repeatedly on the receiving end of extortion calls. From builders to bar owners, no one was spared. On the one hand, Dawood's men were demanding money in increasing amounts. And on the other hand, Rajan, who had split with his master in 1993, had formed his own gang and was also making similar demands.

There was a constant tug of war for power on the streets of the city between the two gangs, in which the rich and the affluent of Bandra and Andheri were becoming the victims. By October 1996, when Sharma was transferred from the ANC to the Khar Police Station in a routine transfer, there was dire need to take some serious steps.

But Sharma's audience with Singh was not only because he was putting together a squad. Singh was aware that Sharma had been transferred to his zone. He would have personally asked for Sharma to be included in his squad if he'd wanted to do so.

However, Firoze Ganjia, who was then Senior Inspector at Khar, was desperate to get Sharma out of his fiefdom. Sharma, who was already famous by this time, was stealing his thunder. Earlier, everyone who came to the police station seeking any kind of help was at Ganjia's mercy. Now people would come asking for Sharma, and Sharma always made it a point to do whatever he could to help them. Duty aside, Sharma had, in his formative years at Mahim Police Station, learned how beneficial it was to help people in trouble because they could, in turn, provide him with solid tips in the future.

When Ganjia heard that Singh was putting a squad together, he saw an opportunity and offered to put in a word for Sharma. Even though Sharma knew what was going on, Sharma let Ganjia act as if he was doing him a favour and went with him to meet Singh.

'You must have heard of him, sir,' Ganjia said, laying it on thick. 'He's conducted so many encounters already.'

Sharma stood at attention and let Singh regard him from head to toe before the latter spoke.

'Are you ready to do this?' Singh asked.

'Yes, sir,' Sharma said firmly.

'Fine. Rohit Verma is your first target.'

There was a moment's silence. Verma was the second in command in the Rajan gang and fiercely loyal to the gangster. He took care of the gang's day-to-day operations, including the extortion rackets, and would personally call businessmen to intimidate them into paying up money.

Sharma knew this was a test. 'Verma is in Bangkok, sir. With Rajan,' he said.

It wasn't just hearsay. Verma really was in Bangkok. Sharma would be proved right four years later when a D-gang squad, led by Munna Jhingada, attacked Rajan in Sukhumvit Soi. Rajan escaped death within an inch, and that was only because Verma threw himself in death's path, taking thirty-two bullets from Jhingada's gun.

Singh laughed. 'Good luck, Sharma.'

The squad, which had four officers and a few constables, started its work in a chowky attached to the Juhu Police Station near Chandan Chowky. It became so famous, making regular headlines in the papers, that it soon became a much sought-after posting for those wishing to bolster their careers. It was not an official posting and cops posted with various police stations in Zone VII were deputed to the squad. Even then, every ambitious cop wanted the chance to say that he had, at some point, worked at Chandan Chowky.

The meeting with Singh that afternoon was pivotal in several ways for Sharma in the future. For one, he met Daya Nayak, his protégé, who too would also garner fame in the future. There were apocryphal stories of how Nayak had worked hard as a waiter in Udipi hotels. He studied to become a police officer in the Mumbai police and then waged a war against the Mumbai underworld. But few knew that he had begun his career with Sharma.

A friend of constable Nitin Vichare, who had posed as a dummy customer in the encounter of Nigerian drug lord Austin Dawson, Nayak went on to give the PSI's exam and got selected as a PSI. Nayak's first brush with policing came in 1993, when he acted as a *panch* (witness) in the case of Dr Imtiyaz Ansari from Kurla. The police, as per law, are required to conduct a *panchnama*—a report signed by five witnesses of panchas—at the scene of the crime before seizing evidence. The panchas are supposed to be independent civilian witnesses and a failure to conduct a panchnama is regarded as a serious violation of law.

After a first couple of postings in rural commissionerates, Nayak was transferred to Mumbai and was posted with the Juhu police. He started angling for a Chandan Chowky stint. An association with Sharma meant accelerated progress. Despite controversies surrounding Sharma, juniors were dying to work with him. At Nayak's insistence, Vichare brought him to meet Sharma, and the latter dismissively said he would keep him in mind.

That opportunity came on 31 December 1996, when Sharma received a tip off about three men from the Rajan gang drinking together at a hotel in the Juhu Gully. As he got off the phone with his informant and turned around, Sharma swore. The Chowky was almost empty, most of the manpower having slipped away to celebrate New Year's Eve.

Hurriedly, he called up PI Nandkumar Mistry, as a senior officer was needed to lead the encounter. Next, he called Juhu Police Station to check who was available. Daya Nayak, who was on night duty, was on the first year of his service, answered the call. Several more calls were exchanged, and battle plans were made, after which all concerned parties rushed to a rendezvous point a couple of buildings away from the hotel.

'Are they still there?' Sharma asked his informant, who had silently come up to the team.

The informant nodded and together, they made their way to the hotel and took positions near the doors. Within minutes, three drunk men stumbled out. The informant just nodded to Sharma and made himself scarce. Sharma gave the pre-decided signal and the police team moved in.

The encounter, in which two of the three henchmen were killed, became Nayak's doorway into his own world of fame as well as controversy. Together, Sharma and Nayak conducted numerous encounters and were also featured in several newspaper and magazine interviews as the latest buddy-pair to hit the encounter scene. Nayak, who has eighty-three kills to his name, was suspended in 2006 after the Anti-Corruption Bureau initiated an inquiry into his assets, but he was reinstated in 2012. In 2015, he was once again suspended for not reporting to his new posting in Nagpur. However, the suspension was revoked in 2016 and he was posted at Amboli Police Station in Mumbai.

The other outcome of Sharma's meeting with Singh was his solid relationship with the superior cop. In 2002, Singh as an Additional Commissioner of north west region Mumbai was up for promotion from deputy inspector general rank to the Inspector General of Police (IGP) rank which would make him eligible to become the joint commissioner in the city police. Sharma, who had worked under him at Chandan Chowky squad, realized that having him head the crime branch would be beneficial for his campaign of the D-gang's decimation. The problem was that Singh was not the only contender and would have to face some serious competition.

By this time, Sharma and Nayak had not only become close to Singh but had also understood the system inside out. They realized that decisions about postings and promotions depended on the officer's merit but only on paper. In reality, there were several influencing factors and the one with the greatest number of influencers on his side took the plum posting.

Over the course of the next several weeks, Sharma and Nayak launched a very subtle campaign for Singh. In those days, social media and its powers had not been invented. Word of mouth or Chinese whispers or European methods of a hush-hush campaign were still the methods that worked best. In these methods, the lobbyists secretly introduced a likely contender and made a noise in other places about how he was the best man for the job, someone who should be kept away because it would spell doom for criminals. The intention behind this was so that the news reached the right ears of the decision makers with the rider (a hidden condition) that all others are good but this particular incumbent despite being first among equals should be kept out. And this invariably tilted the decision in the incumbent's favour.

After conducting a strategically controlled information campaign, Sharma and Nayak realized that the Mantralaya had taken note of this news and was inclined to consider Singh, who was earlier nowhere in the reckoning. Immediately, they changed their track and started a different kind of campaign using a different set of people.

Every politician is surrounded by his own *khaas aadmi* (important men) who perform a variety of duties, from assisting to advising. The best ones become indispensable to the politician. Transfers and promotions in the Maharashtra Police are approved by the state home minister, a post which was held by Chhagan Bhujbal at the time. Sharma and Nayak caught hold of all his khaas aadmis and made it known that Singh becoming the joint commissioner of police of the crime branch would be beneficial to all concerned parties.

The strategy worked and Singh was made the crime branch chief.

Singh, who was known to be a dark horse in the race, was stunned at such a turnaround where he managed to get the posting by leaving all favourites far behind.

Singh was an erudite man. He had dreamed of becoming a scientist but ended up as an IPS officer of 1980 batch. A litterateur and author, Dr Singh, initially found it difficult to acclimatize in the cut-throat world of politics in the Mumbai Police. However, he soon found his feet and fought back. Singh's special squad in Bandra had done quite well and despite being Sharma's senior, he had picked up a thing or two from him.

Dr Singh's elevation as JCP crime was a gamechanger in more ways than any one can imagine. It had earned Sharma a place of trust in Singh's book, a fact that would impact the lives of both Singh and Sharma years later. This also poised Singh for future challenges and bigger positions. Sharma, on the other hand, had one goal—he wanted a powerful Godfather in the force who could back him in his fight against the underworld. A crime branch chief's support would be a major bulwark in his fight against the Dawood gang. He needed this desperately to get one up on Salaskar. And he finally got it.

16

Salaskar's Strategy

Salaskar rolled down the window of his Maruti 1000 with one hand, while absently running his finger over his service revolver with the other. Next to him, in the front passenger seat, his wireless set crackled intermittently. Rajawadi junction was close to Rajawadi Hospital in Ghatkopar and there was a steady flow of both pedestrian and vehicular traffic. A few minutes ago, Salaskar had reached the spot and asked his colleague, SI Subhash Mayekar, to take position further down the road.

That afternoon, in August 1997, was just one chapter in a long story that had begun in the early 1990s when Shiv Sena supremo Balasaheb Thackeray, in a rally at Shivaji Park shortly after the 1992–93 riots, had declared, 'If you [the Muslim community] have Dawood, we have Gawli.'

The late Thackeray's statement may have been a reference to the murder of Dawood's brother-in-law, Ibrahim Parkar, in 1992. Parkar was shot dead by Shailesh Haldankar, Gawli's aide. The murder was Gawli's revenge against Dawood for the murder of his brother Pappa alias Kishore Gawli. The blatant hit on someone so closely related to Dawood—who was already in

Dubai by the time—and that too on his home turf in Nagpada made everyone sit up and take notice. Suddenly, Dawood was no longer a scary name whispered to keep the kids in line. Suddenly, he seemed human. Suddenly, there was someone who could hit him where it hurt without any care about the consequences.

Thackeray, like any good politician, used it to his advantage. His single point agenda was to fan the already burning flame of communal disharmony so that the Hindu votes come rolling in his favour. And so, Thackeray made the statement that further boosted Gawli's image.

A grateful Gawli extended his full support to the Shiv Sena, helping the party organize election rallies and campaigns. In March 1995, the Shiv Sena–BJP alliance defeated the Congress (I) government and came to power for the first time in twenty-nine years.

Perhaps due to Thackeray's statement at the rally, and also because he thought that his efforts in the recent election campaigning had earned him huge favour in the corridors of the Mantralaya, Gawli did something that shocked everyone, be it in the underworld, the police or the government. He applied for police protection.

The decision was not because Gawli was living in a fool's paradise. Fear was an important factor. After all, he had laid a hand directly on Dawood's body, so to speak, and a furious Dawood like any wounded tiger was bound to hit back. In fact, whispers were already rife in the underworld that Dawood had offered a massive reward to anyone who avenged Parkar's murder. What Gawli did not understand was that politicians do not have friends. Everyone is expendable and there are no exceptions.

When Gawli's application made its way up the ranks of the Mumbai Police and reached then Home Minister Gopinath Munde's desk, the latter didn't know whether to laugh or be furious. As he read the file and realized that it was not a practical joke, he dismissed the request and threw the file out.

The development came as a shock to Gawli, who tried to curry favour with Matoshree—the Shiv Sena hub in Kala Nagar in Bandra East. However, nothing worked and within the same month, Gawli was arrested in some minor case and lodged in Harsul Central Jail in Aurangabad.

This sequence of events marked the beginning of a feud that would ultimately lead to the gang's decimation. Gawli made mistake after mistake that led to the Shiv Sena losing its patience with him. His first one attack on the Shiv Sena was also his biggest.

On 30 April 1996, Jayant Jadhav, who was like a *manasputra* (godson) to Thackeray, was shot dead in his Dadar residence. Initially, it was suspected to be the handiwork of the Pandav Putra gang, local hoodlums who had an ongoing vendetta with Jadhav. But there was no evidence, even circumstantial, against them. It took the police some time to figure out that the culprit was Gawli. Even though Gawli was still in jail, he was already plotting his next move. Despite being booked for Jadhav's murder, he managed to secure bail on a technicality. The first thing he did after returning to Dagdi Chawl was to join hands with Jitendra Dabholkar—who was then heading the Shiv Sena's labour wing—and launch his own political party, the Akhil Bharatiya Sena. This was not the ingenuity of a maverick but a war bugle.

This slowly became a headache for the police as well. In fact, in one of the public speeches a joint commissioner of police expressed his apprehensions about Gawli's ambitions. He said that if Gawli were to go legit, he could soon win elections which may lead to him becoming the next home minister of the state government. In such a case, even the police officers would be forced to salute him as their boss. However, the Sena bosses were not going to sit idle and this is where Salaskar came in.

At an off the books meeting between a top Shiv Sena leader and Salaskar, the former promised complete carte blanche if the latter ensured the extinction of the Gawli gang. 'You will get everything you need. Just ensure he doesn't raise his ugly face again,' the leader told Salaskar.

Before he donned the khaki, Salaskar had been a Sena soldier. He identified with their ideals and principles. With the support of the government against a local gang lord, Salaskar did not need anyone else. This was his idea of power. And the strategy worked.

Salaskar would go on to wreak such damage on the Gawli gang that at one point, Gawli approached the state government and requested for Salaskar to be transferred to another city because the cop was out to kill him. Salaskar single-handedly inflicted more damage to the gang than the entire police force.

Salaskar shot dead all the Gawli gang's ace shooters, including Ganesh Vakil, Vijay Tandel and others. According to police records, in 1997, Salaskar alone had eliminated seventeen top aides of the Gawli gang. After which he had concentrated his energies on tracking down Gawli's right hand Sada Pawle, also known as Sada Mama. Even Gawli was a bit scared of Pawle because of his brutish nature and infamous temper.

In fact, Salaskar, despite being so famous, accepted the lowly job of sitting in a chowky because it was opposite Dagdi

Chawl. Salaskar's very presence outside Dagdi Chawl gave Gawli goose bumps.

Salaskar subsequently acquired an AK-47 and began flaunting it while roaming outside Dagdi Chawl. He was playing cerebral judo with Gawli. The idea was that he would soon storm Dagdi Chawl and kill all the criminals, including Gawli. Gawli was so paranoid that he began referring to Salaskar as 'Chakram' (deranged). Gawli began resorting to desperate measures. He formed a protective cordon of women around him because he knew that Salaskar could never open fire on women.

Nevertheless, Salaskar continued his vigil outside Gawli's headquarters. Meanwhile, Gawli got his battery of lawyers to move the High Court and ensure that the court pass strictures against Salaskar and ask him to surrender his AK-47.

This, in turn, set Sharma on his own path. While Salaskar, in a special squad operating under then DCP Zone II Param Bir Singh, went after Gawli, Sharma, working under Satyapal Singh, who was DCP Zone VII at the time, declared a war on Dawood's gang. Today, even his most vehement detractors will agree, even if it is grudgingly, that his encounters were responsible for finishing Dawood's activities in Mumbai.

The axe didn't take long to fall. The police's first move was to arrest Gawli and charge him with the National Security Act (NSA). The police would later wonder why they had even bothered. The whole thing turned into a huge political drama, with Mohan Rawle, a Sena member of parliament, sitting on a hunger strike outside the Agripada Police Station. Rawle and Gawli became heroes in the media and the police. After eight days of the media circus, Gawli was released and returned home amid much jubilation. As the police ground their teeth, Gawli filed a writ petition challenging his arrest. The Bombay High

Court not only ruled in his favour but also came down heavily on the police.

But what finally gave the police the license to kill was the murder of top builder Natwarlal Desai. As if the target himself wasn't big enough, he was shot dead in his office in Nariman Point, a stone's throw away from Mantralaya.

Any disaster that occurs in south Mumbai (re-christened from Bombay by the Sena) always turns out to be the government's worst nightmare. Nariman Point houses the biggest and richest of commercial establishments, not to mention the fact that it is home to many affluent businessmen. In 2009, when the Mumbai Police laid a heavy cordon around the Taj Mahal hotel in the wake of the 26/11 attacks, Colaba residents staged a protest at the Azad Maidan demanding their 'morning walk space' back.

The police took their gloves off. Within a week, all the three shooters—Vijay Muchwa, Vijay Shirodkar and Pankaj Pandey—were shot dead in encounters. Singh's squad also did something that no policeman had dreamt of before—a massive raid on Dagdi Chawl.

That, however, was just the beginning. Now Salaskar was planning to deliver the coup de grace to Gawli. After months of tapping all sources, Salaskar's team had finally learned that Pawle, along with his family members, was on his way to Shirdi and would be passing through the Rajawadi junction, where he was now waiting. If successful, this encounter would break the gang's very backbone. Salaskar's wireless cracked. He picked it up.

'Sir?' PSI Subhash Mayekar reported.

'*Bol*,' Salaskar said.

'I see them coming.'

Salaskar turned the key in the ignition and stepped on the accelerator. This would be the death knell for Gawli gang. At one point, the entire Mumbai police—especially all the encounter specialists like Praful Bhosale, Ravindra Angre and even Pradeep Sharma—was chasing Sada Pawle, but it was Salaskar who got him at the end. Pawle was killed in an encounter in the crowded Ghatkopar east area in the presence of his relatives. This created an uproar among the human rights activists with several petitions pouring into the High Court simultaneously. The Mumbai Police top brass found itself in a tight corner.

17

Sharma's 100 Second Death Knell

As Sharma stepped into the two-room office in the crowded commercial section of Mahim, his face was stony. His mind, however, was raging with fury.

It was September 1997. The man who lay on the floor in a pool of blood was not just one more victim who had fallen prey to gang related violence. This man was his friend. And he had died only because Sharma had been his friend.

Kushalraj Jain was a small-time moneylender operating out of a modest office in Mahim. Sharma first met him while pounding the pavement as a newly joined SI when he was posted at Mahim Police Station and the two men went on to become friends. They stayed in touch even after Sharma was transferred out of Mahim. Whenever his work took him to Mahim or nearby areas, Sharma would make it a point to visit Jain.

As he took in Jain's bullet-ridden body, Sharma turned around and glanced across the street. Among the people gathered just beyond the police cordon was a fast food seller who ran his stall across the street from Jain's office. Sharma loved his *bhajiya*s and had many fond memories of eating them with Jain in the latter's office. The vendor met Sharma's eye just as Sharma looked at him. Sharma saw that the vendor had tears in his eyes.

Sharma just nodded to the vendor and exited the office. Getting into his car, he drove to Chandan Chowky at Juhu, his jaw clenched all the way. As Sharma entered, Daya Nayak saw him and came over. Nayak knew that Sharma was close to Jain.

Before Nayak could say anything, Sharma spoke. 'He was an innocent man, not connected with the underworld in any way,' he said. 'He was killed because I was friends with him.'

Nayak nodded sympathetically. 'What do you want to do?' he asked.

'Go all out, make his killers pay,' Sharma said, his face hardening with every single word.

Jain's murder had its genesis in an order issued by R.D. Tyagi, who was the Commissioner of Police at the time. A little after Sharma joined Satyapal Singh's squad, Tyagi issued orders to ensure that the activities of Chhota Shakeel, which had risen in the western suburbs, needed to be curbed at the earliest.

In August 1997, film producer Gulshan Kumar had been murdered and the entire film industry was in mortal fear of that they would be the next in the underworld's hit list. Kumar's murder caused a massive stir because they could not believe that someone so important could be touched, let alone gunned down. The people's trust in the police was at an all-time low, and the underworld's coffers were overflowing, the fear psychosis having worked its magic. Even businessmen, like those in real estate or the bar industry, paid up whatever they could rustle up every time Shakeel called them. The top brass soon realized that a large chunk of the police force was on Dawood's payroll and perfectly happy to turn a blind eye to the bloodshed on the streets if their money kept coming in. A paradigm shift was needed and a bullet for a bullet was the only answer.

People like Sharma and Salaskar were only too happy to pay the underworld back in its own currency and thus began a spate of encounters that, while initially ignored, finally caused Shakeel to sit up and take notice. Shakeel decided to convey the idea of collateral damage to Sharma in a different way. He made it personal.

He found out about Sharma's friendship with Jain and put his best men on the job. A hit squad led by Sadiq Kaliya and Munna Jhingada barged into Jain's office in Mahim and shot him down in cold blood in broad daylight. The plan was to deter and daunt Sharma by causing bloodshed in his close circles. If Shakeel thought killing Jain was going to put a stop to Sharma's clean-up campaign against him, it was a gross miscalculation.

Shakeel didn't know that by killing Sharma's friend he had begun his gang's decimation. Until then Sharma had been business-like, treating the Shakeel gang as one of the outlaw mafia fraternity. But Jain's death had shaken Sharma. He realized that he needed to hit back and this time with vengeance which would convey his personal angst and professional fury. Now Sharma had a single point agenda. This was not a routine cop-criminal game of one-upmanship anymore. This was an all-out war.

Sharma first put the word out offering a hefty reward for any information related to Jain's murder. As the informants rose to the occasion and the tip offs started trickling in, Sharma was confirmed that Jhingada was involved. He then drew up a list of Jhingada's relatives in the city and leaned hard on them. This tried and tested tactic of the police force always paid dividends. While searching for a wanted accused, the police always call all their relatives, no matter how distant the relation, to the police station or crime branch unit, and make them sit in front of them while hardcore criminals are given the third degree. By the time the officer turns his attention to the family members, they are already terrified due to the sound of the screams of those being interrogated. The officer, almost casually, goes on to tell the relatives that while the wanted accused is going to face the action sooner or later, anyone found to be shielding or harbouring him, too, will not be spared. Those were the days when criminals were being gunned down in encounters left, right and centre and everyone connected to them lived in constant fear of being caught in the crossfire. This was a trick which the Mumbai Police had picked up during the serial blasts of 1993 where the relatives were used as bait to implicate the accused and make them sign the confessional statement under Terrorist and Disruptive Activities Act (TADA). It was called fourth-degree torture, a method perfected by the Mumbai Police.

The tactic worked and one of Jhingada's relatives told Sharma about his whereabouts, after which Jhingada was picked up and brought to the squad's Juhu office. Many policemen would later wonder why Jhingada was picked up alive and not gunned down on the spot. By this time, there had emerged a class of 'encounter specialists' who would pick up gangland foot soldiers, squeeze them for every bit of information without declaring them as officially detained or arrested, and then take them to a remote location where they would be shot dead. The next day, the newspapers would carry the standard template of how the criminal was 'killed in return-fire' after he 'fired at the police when asked to surrender'.

Jhingada, with scores of kills to his name and a fearsome reputation as a top-notch shooter for the D-gang who enjoyed Shakeels' personal affection, was a 'fit customer' for an encounter. Jhingada would go on to lead the hit squad that attacked Chhotta Rajan in Sukhumvit Soi in Bangkok in 2000. But Sharma had the woods in his sights, not the trees. Jhingada, due to the position and respect he enjoyed in the gang, was his key to the gang's entire network in the city as well as outside of it. Sharma's objective was to neutralize the entire gang, not just one sharpshooter.

Using the two imported guns found on Jhingada as basis, Sharma arrested him and obtained maximum police custody. For days on end, Jhingada was interrogated and Sharma made careful note of every bit of information. Patiently, doggedly, he made a detailed map of the entire gang hierarchy.

Unlike military special operation commandoes and elite Marine units who devise a proper battle plan to take on their adversaries, Sharma was a grassroot level officer. However, Jain's killing had shaken him, and his martial instincts took over him.

Sharma had decided to approach this mission as a proper combat and fight it tooth and nail. But he knew he could not do this unless he had his entire team's backing. Sharma needed to inspire his men to meet the challenge with equal intensity. After much thinking and deliberation, Sharma decided to motivate his team the way subjects like Math and Physics are taught at schools and colleges. Why could he not apply the same principles of visualization to galvanize his men into action?

Sharma got a huge white board installed in his office and delegated the responsibility of strategic planning to the best man in his team, Aslam Momin. Momin had best of the legal brains and clarity of thinking strategically under extreme pressure.

Several columns and tables were drawn on the white board. Sharma had kept his chart simple so that even the least educated constables could grasp the idea. It was a unique way to stimulate the men and encourage them to pick up the gauntlet.

On the charts, the main headers comprised all the top lieutenants and managers of Shakeel's gang, with sub heads featuring the names of their financiers, supporters and gang sympathisers, including the names of several city-based builders, Bollywood producers and diamond merchants from Bullion market in Kalbadevi area. In the right-hand corner was a single long column running from top of the board to the bottom, which almost ran across the 15-feet wall, listing the names of Shakeel's many sharpshooters and contract killers wanted in various killings and suspected aides in violent crimes. This was also the best example of ground level intelligence gathering in tackling urban warfare.

Once Sharma was satisfied with his data collection and collation, he called a meeting of his entire team in the office and prepared to address them. Sharma never believed in the concept of meetings. He often joked, '*Sheron ko kabhi conference karte dekha hai, woh sirf shikaar karte hain* (Lions never confer, they only hunt to kill).'

But on that day, Sharma needed to talk to his trusted team for only 100 seconds. Sharma and his legendary 100-second briefings had become a much talked about subject in various police quarters. In fact, several management gurus began talking about it in their motivational lectures. A jovial and smiling Sharma was quite grim on that day. He stood in front of the huge board and began folding up his sleeves. Sharma was always uncomfortable in full sleeved shirts, but he never switched to half sleeves. As Sharma stood looking at the white board, with red and blue markers in his hand, he was reminded of Kushal Jain's smiling face and felt a lump in his throat. His eyes moistened and he felt he would choke. However, he reined in his emotions, cleared his throat and addressed the men in the room.

'I want all of you to look at the names of the people carefully. Here are two categories of people. The column on the left comprise Shakeel's managers and think-tank. I want all of them to be booked, prosecuted, implicated and thrown into jail for as long as the law permits,' he began. 'The second category is the names of his lieutenants and gunmen who pull the trigger at his command. I doubt if we can get them alive...'

Sharma took a long pause. 'To be honest...I am not sure if I am interested in netting them alive,' he said finally.

With this Sharma's well-rehearsed speech was over and his inner most thoughts were made public to his trusted men. Sharma had declared full-fledged war against the Chhota Shakeel gang. Never before had such a systematic and strategically focussed campaign been launched by a single police officer against any organized gang.

Shakeel had not anticipated that killing Sharma's friend would incur his wrath to such an extent that the officer would not rest till he had eliminated every single man connected to the gang. Sharma's philosophy was simple. 'Go for the jugular—drain his money and finish his men.'

A widespread crackdown was planned, and ruthlessly executed daily. No one was spared, no pity was shown. Sharma's office began teeming with people of all hues. This included old couples whose sons had been picked up in nocturnal raids, young worried women whose husbands had not shown up for the past few days and they were told that they had been picked up by Sharma's men, sisters were looking for brothers, middle aged men were concerned about their brothers. The milling crowd were hoping that Sharma would show them some mercy. Sharma refused to meet them or even give them a hearing.

'*Agar woh Dawood ke liye kaam karta hai ... toh mere kaam ka aadmi hai* (If he works for Dawood then he is my work),' he said.

Since most of the families who came to see him were Muslims, Sharma was also dubbed as communally biased, targeting the minority because he himself belonged to a Gaur Sanadya Brahmin clan. Sharma remained heedless to such allegations. Sharma was relentless in his pursuit. There are recordings of intercepted calls in which Shakeel is heard telling his men to be wary of Sharma. 'That Pardeep [that's how he pronounced the name] has gone crazy,' Shakeel would tell his foot soldiers. 'Stay away from Sharma's area. Don't venture beyond the Mahim area. I am working on a way to get him out of the way.'

Time and again, Shakeel sent messages to Sharma through his foot soldiers, offering him everything, including cash, in exchange for leaving his gang members alone. When the first few feelers came in, Sharma made it clear that the only thing that would make him back off was for Shakeel to stop being a nuisance in his city. When Shakeel persisted, Sharma just stopped responding and increased the tempo of his encounters. Shakeel even tried to get his people in the police force to do something about the thorn in his side. But Sharma was not worried because he had the top leadership on his side. Tyagi, and then Mendonca, who took over as CP after Tyagi, made it clear to Sharma that Mumbai was no longer the underworld's playground. Sharma wholeheartedly agreed. But the odds were stacked against the Mumbai Police...

18

Dire Straits

Sharma kicked the chair in frustration.

This was the third time that he had received perfectly credible information but could do nothing about it. The first two times, he had tried to convince Joint Commissioner of Police R.S. Sharma but to no avail.

Pradeep Sharma blamed Salaskar for the manner in which he had killed Sada Pawle in broad daylight which had raised the hackles of human rights activists.

On their way back from the meeting at head office, Daya Nayak had asked Sharma, 'You think this is the end for all of us?'

'I think a few rotten apples have spoiled the entire bloody cart,' Sharma said through gritted teeth, looking out of the vehicle's window.

This time around, Sharma didn't even bother. His informant had sworn that he had sighted a D-gang shooter responsible for at least three shootouts in the city. The shooter had a favourite bar which he frequented regularly. Sharma just gave the informant more money than usual and sent him away.

Pawle was shot down by Salaskar's team in Ghatkopar, while he was on his way to Shirdi with his family. His sister and brother, in a writ that they filed in court, had submitted that Pawle was dragged out of his car with the express intention of being shot down. His sister went on to appeal to the emotions of the judges, saying that she had been clinging to him when he was dragged out, and that Sada Pawle asked her to let him go as he did not want her to pay with her life for his sins.

The year was 1998. Encounter killings had come to a standstill. The gangs were reacting by wreaking hell on the city streets. Foot soldiers were shooting each other, shooting extortion targets or shooting eyewitnesses in broad daylight, knowing that they could now face only arrest and not an encounter. Those like Sharma, who specialized in encounters, now refused to go through the humiliation of arresting someone just to see them walk free in a matter of hours.

By the mid-nineties, the menace of organized crime had spread across the city. Businessmen were wary of helmet clad bikers who stopped too close to their swanky cars at traffic signals, lest the pillion rider pull out a gun and shoot indiscriminately through the tinted windows before zipping away. Actors dreaded visits from unknown, dangerous faces on their movie sets. Producers were coerced to cast certain actors and actresses or face the consequences. Real estate developers were forced to accept partnerships they never wanted in the first place. For the rich and the elite, a call from the *bhai-log* (dons) was terrorizing. The average Mumbaikar went about his day in constant fear of getting caught in the crossfire of the cops and the criminals. People stopped throwing lavish weddings or celebrations lest Mafia hear about it and come calling. Businessmen who bought new and swanky flats kept them a secret so that the dons sitting abroad did not receive the intelligence and start asking for their 'goodwill money'.

It all had started in 1995, when the Mumbai Police developed a 'shoot first, talk later' policy under Commissioner of Police R.D. Tyagi. Encounters were now not just restricted to the Crime Branch; in fact, each zone of Mumbai Police was ordered to shoot down criminals, whether the cops wanted to or not. In 1993, during the communal riots which followed the demolition of the Babri Masjid, Tyagi had ordered his men to storm a bakery in Dongri which led to the death of eight people. And after a spate of robberies that struck the jewellery shops in Zaveri Bazar, he had not hesitated to recommend to the public that they had the Mumbai Police's full support if the public used hockey sticks to beat the robbers (of course in self-defence) to death. Nevertheless, his orders got the ball rolling and encounters became the tool of choice for the Mumbai Police.

Pradeep Sharma and Vijay Salaskar were naturally poised to spearhead this war against the mafia even though the two erstwhile friends were at loggerheads with each other. Tacitly, they had decided to keep out of each other's way in their own personal missions.

After the Black Friday blasts in March 1993, divisions along religious lines started appearing in the underworld. Chhota Rajan claimed to have split from Dawood Ibrahim owing to the latter's involvement in Black Friday. He positioned himself as a patriotic don who was against the enemies of the nation. Dawood's men, especially his lieutenant Chhota Shakeel, have repeatedly claimed that Rajan's story was hollow rhetoric because Rajan had worked for the Company for an extended period even after the blasts. Then Shiv Sena chief Bal Thackeray had also lent political colour to the divide in the mafia by claiming that Arun Gawli's gang were *aamchi muley* (our boys) and a deterrent to Dawood Ibrahim's clout.

In order to decimate Gawli, Salaskar not only shot down Gawli's men but employed other approaches to finish his clout. Salaskar and his officers began counselling the youngsters of Dagdi Chawl—Arun Gawli's fortress—that death was certain if they chose to work as hitmen for Gawli. Parents who were once proud that their wards were gun-toting gangsters began fearing for the lives of their children.

Pradeep Sharma, on the other hand, went after Dawood Ibrahim's gang. At the time, he was working with Zone VII which covered Bandra to Andheri. The dreaded don, who was shuttling between Dubai and Karachi, seethed in rage each time one of his men fell to Sharma's bullets.

On 12 August 1997, music baron Gulshan Kumar was shot at the stairs of a Shiv temple in Mumbai. The murder was suspected to be the work of Abu Salem. The Government of Maharashtra, and the Mumbai Police, was under severe pressure from the business community to respond. The Mumbai Police's investigations revealed that Javed Fawda was one of the three shooters involved in Gulshan Kumar's murder. On 28 August, weeks after Gulshan's murder, assistant police inspector Vasant Dhoble headed an encounter and claimed to have shot down Javed Fawda near Ballard Pier. It made news for all the wrong reasons.

The encounter was later recreated with a different version pieced together by eyewitnesses summoned by human rights activists in the court. The Aguiar report states that on the afternoon of 26 August, a man called Abu Sayama had finished praying at a local mosque when a police vehicle pulled up outside.[3] The policemen grabbed Sayama as soon as he stepped outside. Sayama's family scoured police stations across the city for more than a week to locate him. A missing person's complaint was also filed. But the police seemed totally disinterested in tracing Sayama. About a week later, Sayama's sister was called to a morgue and asked to identify a dead body. The condition of the body made it obvious that the deceased had been subjected to vicious torture. His chest and torso were covered with the tyre marks of a heavy vehicle. He had been shot at close range multiple times. To her horror, she was told that the body belonged to Javed Fawda, a dreaded criminal who had shot Gulshan Kumar. Nothing was farther than the truth, she claimed. Her brother was Abu Sayama, a peanut vendor who would set his shop outside railway stations every day to feed his family and take care of their mother was suffering from cancer.

The poverty ridden conditions of Sayama's family generated public sympathy. Human rights associations went red with rage. The policemen were accused of being the judge, jury and executioner. It was also during this period that the traditional 'script' of an encounter became commonplace. 'The police cornered the gangster based on intel. The gangster opened fire and was shot in retaliation. He was rushed to the hospital but pronounced dead on arrival.'

But cases like Sayama and Sada Pawle began to raise doubts over the police's version of events. Why was the man shot multiple times? Why were there tyre marks appear all over the victim's body? The local unit of the Samajwadi Party also took

[3] 'The Aguiar Commission Report on the Extra Judicial Executions by the Bombay Police', Bombay Police, 9 May 2013. http://www.oocities.org/indianfascism/fascism/bombay1.htm

up the Fawda case to raise their voice against police atrocities. It didn't help that the cop who pulled the trigger was glorified in the media.

There were cops who viewed encounters as a shortcut to success. Earlier, only top gangsters were encountered by the police, but now even lower rung leaders were getting killed. Each encounter specialist was also keeping a 'score'—the number of criminals he had killed—and some of the overzealous cops would throw parties to celebrate their half centuries. Rivalries came into play, with some cops pressing the trigger to keep their score moving. Newspaper reports often carried articles with photographs of the cops posing in style with their guns. Pictures of policemen wearing sports shoes and squatting next to the bodies of the gangsters they had killed became commonplace. These visuals posed a question to society at large—Even if encounters were a necessity, was there a need to celebrate them like a birthday party? This was one of the most difficult periods for the Mumbai police.

Soon human rights activists filed PIL after PIL with the Bombay High Court, seeking inquiries into all encounters, past and present, and a total ban on them, claiming that it went against the very basic human rights of the victims. Urban lawyers wrote petitions to the National Human Rights Commission (NHRC) terming these encounters as extra judicial killings. Allegations surfaced that different cops were also working in collusion with different mafia bosses and bumping off gang rivals they were in cahoots with.

A petition demanded a CBI inquiry into Fawda's encounter and another to look into Sada Pawle's encounter, which had been conducted by Salaskar. Judge A.S. Aguiar of the Sessions Court was appointed by the High Court to probe into the two encounters in 1998. Judge Aguiar examined the evidence of the encounters and cross-examined the officers and the witnesses involved. He concluded that the two encounters were fake. The media termed the report as a hard rap on the knuckles for the Mumbai Police as well as the Maharashtra government helmed by the alliance of the Shiv Sena and the BJP, which was due to face elections in the next calendar year.

A division bench of the Bombay High Court heard a series of litigations and at every hearing, the bench would come down hard on the police about the brutality of the encounters. Reporters, who had once gleefully covered the escapades of their favourite cops and curried favours with them, were now running articles with quotes from civilian experts about the veracity of the encounters.

Naturally, the encounter cops became averse to pulling the trigger now. Even Sharma and Salaskar holstered their guns. The very word 'encounter' became taboo and efforts were made to change the term to 'operation'. However, previously each encounter had served as a deterrent for the hundreds of wannabes who were dreaming of becoming shooters for the underworld. That deterrent was now missing. No sooner had the cops been ordered to hold back than the mafia raised its ugly head again. Shootouts became rampant in the city. In 1998, there were nearly 100 reported instances. The mafia became so emboldened that one shootout was being reported every three days on an average. Things were back to square one.

Now, the Government of Maharashtra was once again under pressure to get law and order back on track! The Mumbai Police had their hands tied by the court, and thus filed a petition against the findings of Judge Aguiar's report in the High Court.

The division bench of Bombay High Court who heard the petition finally rejected the Aguiar report. Aloysius Aguiar was the Sessions judge who had submitted a 200-odd page report declaring Javed Fawda and Sada Pawle's encounters as fake.[4] This time, a division bench of the High Court found that the encounters of Javed Fawda and Sada Pawle were genuine. Emboldened by the High Court judgement, the encounter cops began cleaning their dusty revolvers once again.

Then police commissioner Ronnie Mendonca called a reporter from the *Indian Express* and in an uncharacteristic gesture agreed to give him an exclusive interview. The next day, the newspaper carried the headline: 'Mendonca's battle cry'.[5] It was a declaration of war against the underworld and a green light for encounters.

Sharma was elated. All his men who were withdrawn from round the clock vigilance on the Shakeel gang were asked to resume their positions once again. The process of judicial inquiry had forced Sharma to suspend his ongoing crackdown against the gang lord. But Mendonca's clear cut proclamation was enough for Sharma to renew his efforts and revitalize his men to go after Shakeel's brood in the city.

---

4 People's Union For Civil . . . vs The State Of Maharashtra & Others on 22 February 1999 1999 (4) BomCR 608.

5 S. Hussain Zaidi, 'Mendonca's battle cry,' *Mumbai Newsline, Indian Express*, 12 May, 1998.

19

The 100-Crore Club

At the Leela Kempinski Hotel, Pradeep Sharma was seated on a wooden bench in the aisle of the club and tying the laces of his sports shoes. He was admiring the spotless flooring when a young businessman from a prominent Mumbai family stepped up and greeted him heartily. Sharma responded in good spirits. The two men had recently got acquainted at a party in the same hotel. Ever since, they would exchange customary pleasantries on sighting each other.

'How about a game?' the businessman asked, spinning the squash racquet in his hand.

'Not today,' Sharma said politely as he had planned on a work-out at the gym.

'Oh, come on,' the businessman said and winked. 'I could teach you a thing or two about squash.'

Sharma resisted the smile which had begun to spread across his face. He apprised the businessman, who was almost a decade younger to him, from head to toe. The young man was smirking with confidence. Sharma was pretty fit himself but at forty-five, age had begun catching up with him. But how could he resit a challenge, especially one which smacked of one-upmanship? He unzipped his black duffle bag and pulled out his squash racquet.

The two men entered the enclosure of the court. Over the next fifteen minutes, Sharma dominated the court like a master player. He read the game way ahead of his opponent. He smashed the butyl rubber ball to the front wall with panache. The businessman was taken aback by the ease with which Sharma was retrieving his shots. Sharma's angled shots often fell beyond the businessman's reach. His drops were top notch. Sharma more than made up for his lack of speed with his acumen and tactical play. At the end of the game, the businessman was left gasping for breath. Sharma had won without too much of a bother.

'Fuck!' the businessman said and wiped the sweat dripping off his face with a hand towel. 'Where did you learn to play like that?'

Long before *Ghajini* became the first Bollywood movie to cross the 100-crore mark at the box office in 2008, there existed another exclusive club which allegedly consisted of policemen who were worth more than a hundred crores. It was called the '100-crore club'. The term was used in a prominent national newspaper with the headline that Pradeep Sharma had been elevated to this club.

Encounter cops have prominently featured in the media for amassing wealth disproportionate to their known sources of income. A famous encounter cop of the 83 batch was alleged to have owned a stake in a prominent theme park which was operational in the city. The cop had also served in the same belt in which the park was located. The theme park had many gravity defying rides which were certainly not for the faint-hearted but not many knew that the investment had come from an inspector of police with a known income of less than a few lakhs a year. Among other things, this cop had reportedly made a lot of money by collecting an unofficial bounty. A businessman in the city had been killed over extortion money by a gangster. The close-knit business community pooled their resources to put up a bounty on the criminal's head. The gangster himself was known for his ferociousness and no cop was eager to go after him. This cop not only took out the gangster but also most of his top associates and virtually finished off the gang. And thus, he was rewarded in no small measure by the business community. One of these encounter specialists also allegedly had a five-star hotel in Kuala Lumpur in Malaysia.

Another cop of the 83 batch may not have had the maximum number of encounters to his name but his numbers in the 100-crore club reportedly exceeded the others. He had allegedly purchased the lease of a state-owned club for ninety-nine years. The security deposit for such a property itself ran into eight figures. This cop's posting in Thane during a boom period in the real estate sector led to huge property gains for him. He was made a partner in several real estate projects. This arrangement suited both the real estate lobby and the cop himself. The builders did not have to fear extortion calls from the mafia as the fearsome cop was already onboard the project. And the cop could purchase multiple properties at discounted prices.

Another encounter specialist had migrated to Mumbai from the rural areas of Udupi in Karnataka. He initially worked at a hotel before qualifying for the PSI exams and joining the Mumbai Police. Such fame and fortune came his way that he constructed a world class school in his native village which was inaugurated in a grand function by some of Bollywood's biggest stars. This cop was later arrested on charges of corruption but was finally released as no evidence was found against him.

It is alleged that some encounter cops made a quick buck by sometimes sparing the man to be encountered in return for money. Also, there were charges that the cops would stow away cash and other valuables from the encounter site. In the famous shootout at Lokhandwala, a mafia boss had allegedly tipped off the police that Maya Dolas, a top gangster, was Dolas' to kill, the fame was theirs to revel in and the huge chunk of cash they would find at Swati Apartments was theirs to keep. It was reported in a popular newspaper that seventy lakhs of cash went missing from the flat which had been used by Maya Dolas as a hideout.

Some encounter specialists also found innovative ways to cover their tracks. One specialist would reportedly leave all aspects of managing his finances in the hands of his ladylove, who was a public prosecutor at the time.

The membership of the club at Leela Kempinski was beyond Pradeep Sharma's middle-class income. Few knew how Sharma had acquired this membership. The Leela Group of Hotels was owned by Captain C.P. Krishnan Nair. When the underworld started troubling the entrepreneur, he approached the police for help. Pradeep Sharma ensured that the case was resolved in time and the threatening calls were stopped. Captain Nair was keen on rewarding Sharma. But Sharma did not want any money for the job. At the Captain's insistence, Sharma became a lifetime member of the club at Leela Kempinski. Here he trained under a professional squash coach for months, and thus was able to beat the young businessman who had challenged him to a game. Sharma also used this opportunity to work out at the gym regularly and keep himself fit.

The Leela Kempinski was situated close to the airport and right in the centre of the city. Sharma was left impressed by the exquisite interiors of the property and the sparkle of the luxurious swimming pool. His close acquaintance with Captain Nair also earned him regular invites to the parties at the five-star hotel.

These splashy parties which featured Mumbai's rich and famous left Sharma totally bedazzled. At these events he felt important because even though these people were rich, they looked up to him and often thought of him as their saviour from the gangsters. Sharma savoured that aura and the clout he wielded among the city's wealthy.

At such parties, Sharma was often personally introduced by Captain Nair to other affluent businessmen and entrepreneurs of the country. Most of these businessmen were worth more than 100 crores and Sharma was regularly seen shaking hands with them at the Leela. In a way, he had broken into an exclusive club. So, the whisper circles were aloud with the news that Sharma was moving around in the 100-crore club. And soon an article reported that Sharma was a part of the 100-crore club because of his wealth. Sharma was clearly affected by the report because only he had been singled out. Sharma felt that the reporter had some deep grouse against him.

It was a matter of pride for Captain Nair that a famous policeman was a patron of his hotel. For Sharma, the arrangement provided him with an opportunity to witness a lifestyle that he could not have dreamed of. For an hour or so that he frequented the club, Sharma would play a few games of squash or use the treadmill to take his mind off.

That day, after the game, Sharma showered and dressed in his formal attire in the changing rooms. Then he stepped outside and watched the city go about its business. An airplane seared into the Mumbai skyline from the nearby airport. Traffic snarled across the congested roads. The streets needed to be free of crime and the dreaded criminals.

And with that thought, Pradeep Sharma was back to being a policeman and detecting one of the many cases he was working on.

20

Lashkar's Quixotic Xanadu

The policemen helped each other fasten their bulletproof jackets as their jeep sped to Goregaon, a north western suburb of Mumbai. Sharma and Nayak rechecked their AK-47 rifles to ensure they were working and ready to spew fire. They kept the magazines out of the rifles to ensure that no one got hit by mistake. None of them could afford a mishap like this, not with where they were going.

This was a serious mission and there was no way that Sharma and his team wanted to return unsuccessfully the way they had returned last time when they had gone to arrest an alleged kingpin and returned with massive embarrassment.

The journey that was taking Sharma and his team to Goregaon had begun with Saquib Nachan; the only criminal who could boast of having crossed paths with Sharma and lived to tell the tale.

Nachan, now a convict in the 2003 Mulund bomb blast case, had been on the police's radar for quite some time. A resident of the Padgha village on the Mumbai Nashik highway, Nachan is today something of a local hero in his village.

His life, and criminal career, are firmly interwoven with the history of Padgha and the neighbouring Borivali village. Until 1970 Hindu and Muslims coexisted peacefully in both villages. Then, according to local lore, the Hindus set an entire forest adjoining the villages on fire. The motive was to bring the Muslims, who depended on the forest for their livelihood, to their knees, and the motivation, according to the Muslims of Padgha, was from the Shiv Sena. Nachan was in school when the incident occurred, and it set him on a path that would eventually land him in Sharma's cross hairs.

The fire was the straw that broke the camel's back. For years, ever since the Shiv Sena was founded, Nachan had been hearing about unspeakable atrocities committed against Muslims in various parts of the Thane district. When he came home from school to find the fire burning and his entire family crying bitterly, it set another fire burning inside him.

From childhood to youth, Nachan quietly nursed that fire till he was introduced to the Salafist form of Islam. The radical ideas propagated by Salafists fanned the embers in his heart, and soon Nachan, whose father had once hosted Sarojini Naidu in his house, had signed up to be part of the Students' Islamic Movement of India (SIMI), an organization that eventually led to the formation of the Indian Mujahideen.

SIMI sent a young and eager Nachan to Pakistan for training and the frequent trips made him a person of interest for Indian intelligence agencies. They kept tabs on him and passed on whatever they had to the Maharashtra police. As standard operating procedure, the police decided to watch him till he caused some harm.

Then, in March 2003, a bomb exploded in a Karjat bound local train while it was crossing the Mulund station.

Eleven people died in the blast and over eighty were injured. This was the third blast in a period of four months. Earlier, in January, a bomb had gone off in a train at Vile Parle, and in December 2002, a bomb had exploded at Mumbai Central. All investigations pointed to the involvement of the Lashkar-e-Taiba (LeT). Instructions were issued straight from the Prime Minister's Office (PMO). Enough was enough.

Central and state intelligence agencies shared dossier after dossier on any man, woman or child who was a person of interest. Nachan's name was high up on the list. Satyapal Singh's team was asked to bring him in. The team was chosen because intelligence clearly indicated that he enjoyed immense support from Padgha residents and might not come as quietly as the average underworld sharpshooter.

A team comprising Pradeep Sharma, Sachin Waze, Daya Nayak and others left from Padgha, armed with their service pistols. It took over an hour to reach Padgha from Bandra and every cop was aware of a tingling sensation in their nerves as they got off their vehicles. The intelligence they had was fairly detailed and locating Nachan's house was not too difficult. In fact, they were glad about not having to ask around for his address, as that would have caused immediate uproar among the people.

Deciding to move quickly, they knocked on Nachan's door, identified themselves and firmly started leading him to their vehicle as fast as they could. They were, unfortunately, not fast enough.

Some locals had been watching the officers as soon as they stepped out of their cars. The people of Padgha were not exactly new to policemen picking them up. They had been dealing with communalism disguised as police procedure for decades, and the fact that 95 per cent of the police force consisted of Maharashtrian personnel who were further stoked by the Shiv Sena's speeches and articles only added fuel to the fire. Living with this had instilled in the Padgha residents a radar that could spot a cop from a mile away.

Almost in unison, several voices were raised, and even as Nachan was bundled inside the van, around fifty people ran toward it and surrounded the vehicle.

'Where are you taking him?' they demanded. 'Let him go immediately!'

The commotion attracted the other residents' attention. The afternoon namaz of Asr had just ended and people were coming back home in large numbers. One look at the police van and they all ran towards it. Within minutes, the van was surrounded by over 500 people.

As Sharma and Nayak settled down in their seat, Nayak said, 'Sir!'

Sharma, who was looking out of the window, gun raised, responded without turning.

'What?' he asked.

'Where's Nachan?'

Sharma turned around to stare at Nayak. Then he looked around the van. Nachan was gone.

The fiasco at Padgha did not go down well for several reasons. This was a case that was a top priority for the government, both state and central. Letting someone as important as Nachan slip through their fingers brought a lot of negative publicity for the entire squad. Rivals were quick to rub it in their faces, either directly or through smear campaigns, which were equally effective.

Sharma and his team responded with urgency. In less than a week, the team returned with reinforcements and descended on Nachan's house. A tight cordon of armed policemen stood outside the house, daring the people to start something. Nachan was long gone, but the team went through every single item in the house for clues about his whereabouts or activities. In an inner room, hidden under reams of literature, was a diary. Sharma was leafing through it when Daya stepped in.

The heap of documents and seized effects were taken to Mumbai along with the diary and other paperwork found in the house. For days on end, the team studied the paperwork and scanned it for clues.

'Here's something we could start with,' Aslam Momin said to Sharma while poring over the diary. Momin, another graduate of the batch of 83, had recently been transferred to the Bandra unit. The presence of a Muslim cop among a predominantly Hindu police force was reassuring for Muslim citizens. However, for the Muslim cops it was a double-edged sword because they could not be biased towards their community while any slip up would only make them look like they had displayed partisan attitude.

Momin pointed to a list of three names and addresses in Kalyan. These were the only specific entries among a sea of vague ones in the diary. It took the team half the day to find photocopies of identity documents corresponding to the names. It was as curious as it was useful because it was the only concrete clue that the police could follow.

Fully aware of Nachan's ties, the team worked on the assumption that their lead was going to be serious and needed a careful approach. Discreetly, the team visited the area of the addresses. Over a period of several days, they made friends among the local know-alls—the barbers, grocers and milkmen who had all the area gossip. Patiently, yet consistently, the team worked out that the three men had recently come to stay in a flat on rent, and that they kept mostly to themselves. Attempts by neighbours to ask the three men about their past addresses were also quickly discouraged by them. As the information started coming in, the creases on the investigators' forehead started deepening. The three men fit the profile of terrorists sent on a mission. Either that, or they were hiding some terrible criminal past. The new local informants were paid to keep an eye out for the trio and keep the team informed about their movements.

Finally, on 21 March 2003, the team had enough to go on. Approval was quickly sought and obtained, and the team raided the flat in Kalyan. It was empty.

The frustrated team pulled out all stops. Raids were conducted at Padgha and Bhiwandi based on intelligence inputs but yielded no results.

On 29 March, Sharma and Nayak were in their office when the phone rang. It was one of their top informants with confirmed information. Two of the suspects were going to Goregaon to meet someone and would be waiting near the highway. Goregaon has pockets of Muslim ghettos where it is possible to melt into the crowd and go totally unnoticed. Sharma slammed the receiver into its cradle and started shouting out orders. Within minutes, Sharma, Nayak, Dnyanesh Devade and Prakash Bhandari were getting ready to leave when Satyapal Singh called.

'Delhi says to be very careful. These men could be armed, and they are extremely motivated,' Singh told Sharma. The latter thanked his superior and hung up.

Going to the armoury, he took bulletproof jackets and passed them around. There was a short disagreement because approaching the suspects with the jackets on would be as good as standing in front of them in full police uniform. Sharma said he was perfectly aware of that and they would simply have to figure it out.

Finally, Sharma and Nayak hefted two AK-47 assault rifles, which were a recent addition to the police armoury. Despite the seriousness of the situation, both cops could not help but feel excited. They had been itching to use the rifles ever since they got them.

'I see them!' Bhandari called from the front passenger seat.

'How do we do this?' Devade asked.

'Get as close as you can safely. Then we approach them on foot,' Sharma replied.

The jeep slowed down and crawled towards the three men who were standing next to a Maruti van. One of them noticed the jeep and kept his eye on it.

'Do it,' Sharma said, and they all sprang out of the jeep.

The officers' movement seemed to be choreographed in unison. The suspects, seeing the movement, ducked inside the van.

Sharma read his intentions. 'Take cover!' he yelled and everyone rushed behind the jeep just as the man, later identified as Abu Sultan, came out with an AK-47 of his own and let loose a barrage of rounds, while the other two, Iqbal Wani and Abu Anwar Ali, opened fire with 9mm pistols. But they were not quick enough. Nayak took a round in the torso but was saved by his vest. He stumbled due to the impact of the round crashing into him, but Sharma caught him and helped him behind the jeep.

Hell broke loose on the highway as people abandoned their vehicles and started running for their lives. Screams of terror mixed with the sound of gunfire. The cops crouched behind the jeep till there was a break in the firing and then, together they returned fire. Finally, after two to three more minutes of exchanging bullets, there were no more gunshots from the Maruti van. The police team waited for a full minute before leaving their cover and slowly advancing towards the van.

All the three men were dead. Sharma called out, saying someone should inform control room. He and Nayak advanced towards the vehicle to make sure no one else was hiding.

It took over two hours to officially take custody of the vehicle. No one had the patience to take it to the unit first, so the team searched it on the spot. The first thing to be found was a stack of documents, which Sharma took with him and found a quiet spot on the pavement. He was at the last page, studying it with increasing incredulity, when Nayak came up to him.

'We found a large amount of cash. Must be three to four lakhs,' he told Sharma, whose eyes were still wide.

Nayak asked him what was wrong. Sharma passed him the documents. The last page was a hand drawn map. Anyone who had worked in Mumbai could identify the target based on the locations marked around it.

The target was Matoshree, Balasaheb Thackeray's house in Bandra.

Both cops sank to the pavement and sat down. A wave of worry passed over their faces.

And then they both begun smiling. They had just averted a major catastrophe—an attempt on Sena Supremo Bal Thackeray's life.

The attack planned by Muslims would have resulted in a major calamity, giving rising to communal conflagration. No one would have bothered checking whether the men were terrorist or simply local Muslim youths.

Subsequently, a team of police officers and men raided Padgha again and recovered a sack from a well. It was laid on the ground and opened to reveal hand grenades. In all, 200 grenades were recovered, an indication of the nefarious planning and preparation.

This encounter put Sharma leagues above other officers and peers. Sharma's friends who once called him 'Bhai' now added the agnomen of respect and began referring to him as 'Baba'. When a visitor once asked a constable in his office why Sharma Sahab had been rechristened Baba, the constable replied that the word meant 'father'. 'Our *saab* is actually the *baap* [father] of all bhais, hence we call him Baba.'

21

Sharma's Powerplay against Shakeel

Sharma laughed. Next to him, Daya Nayak was smirking. In fact, every cop in the room was amused. On the table between them, a cellular call interception instrument was connected to a speaker. The instrument was relaying the entire conversation between the two callers to the room that the Criminal Intelligence Unit (CIU) squad used for interception.

On a phone call from Dubai, Chhota Shakeel had just finished outlining his plans to extort some top Bollywood figures in great detail. Every part of the plan, ranging from logistics to manpower involved was discussed, much to the obvious discomfort of the man in Mumbai who was listening at the other end. Time and again, he tried to cut in and interrupt his boss, who droned on nonetheless with zero regard to any form of discretion.

Sharma and his team had a fair idea why the Mumbai based foot soldier was so nervous, and they could not contain their laughter as they took notes.

'Bhai ... bhai may I say something?' the lieutenant ventured. 'Bhai, it might not be a good idea to talk in such detail. The police are now tapping phones. Many of the people we gave orders to on the phone have disappeared. And turned up dead the next day as encounter victims…'

'*Arrey tu tension mat le* (Don't you worry),' Shakeel boasted. 'Now write this number down.'

A constable in the room had to stand up and turn away as he was chortling too hard. Sharma, too, was holding his head with one hand while his shoulders shook. The tech savvy D-gang were among the first to make use of technological advances for their work, be it pagers, cell phones or emails. But being tech savvy and being smart, as Pradeep Sharma soon discovered, were two very different things.

Since the time Sharma had waged war against the D-gang after his friend Kushal Jain's murder in 1997, Sharma was leading a two-pronged assault on Shakeel. One aspect focussed on old fashioned police work which included human intelligence and picking up suspects for the good old third degree. The other aspect focused on breaking into the gang through electronic surveillance.

When two to three D-gang foot soldiers were found to be carrying pagers at the time of their arrest, the squad realized that the gang had switched from passing contact numbers on handwritten notes to pagers. Sharma and Satyapal Singh had a meeting with the Home Department, seeking permission to start intercepting the pagers. The government granted permission to intercept electronic communication as long as it had reason to believe that the targets were indulging in anti-national activities. And after 1993, the entire D-gang was labelled anti-national.

The next step in the plan was much more challenging. Sharma's squad drew up a list of all public telephones in secluded areas from Dadar to the western suburbs. The squad was operating on the assumption that gang members would not choose crowded places to discuss their activities, where people waited impatiently in long queues. Phones enclosed in glass booths were given special preference. The list was painstakingly made over a month, when scores of constables pounded the pavement and gathered numbers of all the public phones that fit the bill. Sharma's men had identified over eighty-five public call offices (PCOs), as they were called, or phone booths that were shortlisted as favourites of the Shakeel gang lieutenants. Once the list was ready, the squad was split up in teams and stationed at strategic locations along the Western and Eastern Express Highways. The spots were chosen because of their proximity to as many of the PCOs on the list.

Then the waiting began. From morning till night, the teams would wait at their assigned spots, while Sharma stayed glued to the intercepting machine. From the arrested gang members picked up earlier, the squad already had a long list of pager numbers being used by other gang members, and all of those were being intercepted.

Soon enough, results started coming in. Every time a gang member got paged with a number to be called, the number would be looked up on the list. If it was on the list, Sharma would convey the information to the team closest to the phone. Scores of D-gang members were either arrested or killed using this approach; Sadiq Kaliya was in the second category—the ones who needed to be killed, not arrested.

As the years passed, pagers were replaced by cell phones and the police's work became both easier and harder at the same time. Now the police could simply intercept the calls and get first-hand information. But at the same time, getting numbers of the gang members would require additional time and effort, and the D-gang was a multi-million-dollar crime syndicate which could afford multiple cell phones for its men.

The process of examining Call Detail Records (CDRs) as a tool for investigation—which is widely prevalent in the police force today—was first adopted during this time. The squad obtained CDRs of the few known contact numbers for D-gang members that were available through informants and drew up a list of the frequently dialled numbers, which were all intercepted. CDRs were then obtained for those numbers which turned out to indeed belong to gang members and the list expanded.

Interception of cellular calls also opened a whole new can of worms. Not only were the mafia moneybags and *hawala* (money launderers) operators exposed, it also shed light on the Bollywood–underworld nexus. In the charge sheets that were later filed against the likes of producer Nazim Rizvi and financier Bharat Shah, the police submitted many hours of transcripts in which Rizvi and Shakeel were heard discussing the casting of top-notch actors in Rizvi's film *Chori Chori Chupke Chupke*. Until then, Rizvi had produced three films, all of them B-grade movies, that released and bombed without any impact. *Chori Chori Chupke Chupke* was different. Rizvi first tried to get Shah Rukh Khan and Hrithik Roshan to act as the male lead. Both actors were threatened endlessly by Shakeel till they finally approached the police. Ultimately, Rizvi was picked up from his Seven Bungalows residence in December 2000, after which the entire unholy nexus came spilling out.[6]

---

[6] Bureau, 'Film Producer Nazim Rizvi Arrested for Underworld Connection', Zee News, 12 December 2000 https://zeenews.india.com/home/film-producer-nazim-rizvi-arrested-for-underworld-connection_5742.html (accessed 3 June 2019).

Cell phones became a huge tool for the D-gang in their business of intimidation. Henchmen would drop in at film sets and meet actors, after which they would make a call on their cell phones and pass the phones to the film people with Shakeel on the other end. There was no need to call a landline multiple times and cell phones were dispensable.

When Shakeel finally understood what his men were trying to tell him—that using cell phones was not a safe option for his gang members—he moved on to the next medium—email. But Sharma was ready. By this time, he had planted a wide range of informants at various levels of the gang and it took him only a few days to learn that the D-gang was now communicating via email. It took him a few more days to get Shakeel's email id. Predictably, Shakeel was only using a single email account. Sharma, with due blessings from his superiors, engaged the services of a civilian hacker and got into Shakeel's email account. On instructions from the same hacker, Sharma left the unread emails alone. Marking a 'read' email as 'unread' was not a feature that had been introduced yet and opening the new email could have alerted Shakeel or his mail managers.

Instead, Sharma accessed the emails Shakeel had sent to his men so that he could find out what orders had already been issued. He was amused, and surprised, to find that Shakeel was once again outlining his plans in vivid detail, this time in writing.

Sharma called the rest of his men and asked them to come to his cabin. He then began unravelling his detailed and strategic plan that he had decided to unleash against the Shakeel gang. Every team member was given a role and some responsibility to contribute towards the mission. All intelligence channels were opened discreetly on a need-to-know basis. Special permissions were obtained, and real time concessions were procured.

The subsequent action by Sharma and his squad has gone down in the annals of history as the most concerted and successful operation conducted by any police unit against Shakeel and his gang. Of the 111 people that Sharma killed in his career, around sixty-five to seventy men, including the hated Sadiq Kaliya, were part of Shakeel's crew, while the rest were Chhota Rajan's men, drug peddlers, dacoits and other criminals. Similarly, among the 1111 people that Sharma arrested in his entire career, over 800 belonged to the Dawood Ibrahim–Chhota Shakeel gangs while the rest were from splinter groups of Chhota Rajan and other minions.

The Shakeel gang never faced so much violence and crackdown since its inception. Perhaps Sharma would have never turned away his attention from Shakeel gang but for two reasons. Firstly, not many top aides or lieutenants were left in the gang. Most of them were either killed, imprisoned or made to flee abroad. Secondly, Sharma began to concentrate on Chhota Rajan's gang after he dared to kill his friend, Amjad Khan, outside the Sessions Court in Mumbai.

After a few years, even though Sharma diverted his attention to other organized gangs and syndicates, and brought them down as well, the Sharma–Shakeel feud would remain permanently etched in the minds of police, underworld and also the news media because Sharma's thirteen-year crusade virtually demolished the gang.

22

Rajan Ravaged

A container ship's horn rang aloud in the distance. The gentle tide of the Arabian sea swayed against the wharves. On a warm summer morning in May 2005, at the Nhava Sheva Docks, Sharma squatted close to one of the several three-feet tall oil drums lined up in front of him. He felt the drums with his hands. He tapped his knuckles against the metal of the container and listened. Then he moved on to the next drum and repeated the exercise until the echoes of suspicion rebounded in his ears. His eyes lit up. He turned towards a constable from his team and pointed at the barrel.

'Open it,' Sharma said and stood up.

A plug on the lid was opened. On Sharma's instructions, the constable dipped a wooden stick inside the plug. When the stick re-emerged out of the barrel, its bottom end was slick with grease. Sharma shook his head as the grease dripped to the floor. Something was amiss. He thumped his palm on the drum's non-removable lid.

'Cut it open,' Sharma ordered.

Quickly, a barrel cutter was arranged, and the sound of scraping metal filled the air as the lid was pried open. Then, Sharma asked his men to empty out the container. Halfway through the exercise, he finally found what he was looking for. He looked upon the catch with the eyes of a treasure hunter who'd found a trove hidden inside the deepest pit of the earth. Behind him, his team craned their necks, trying to get a good view.

Investigators around the world often crack significant cases by an element of luck. Similarly, the biggest investigation case in Sharma's professional life was not an outcome of diligent detection but merely a matter of chance. However, it was a windfall of sorts, and it was all because Sharma decided to follow his instincts. This case left Sharma incredulous with disbelief as minimal efforts yielded massive results.

The spectacle in front of the crime branch team that morning was the result of a sequence of events that started three months ago. Sharma, as always, was on the lookout for new cases. That meant employing all the tricks he had learned so far. He would go about lubricating the supply chain of the khabri network with fat wads of currency from the Informers' Secret Fund, leaning on history sheeters for news of crimes brewing in the city's underbelly, intercepting phone calls through wiretap or electronic surveillance and conducting surprise raids and checks at random hideouts of known gangsters.

The raid that led Sharma to the Jawaharlal Nehru Port Trust (JNPT) at Nhava Sheva docks was the result of a tip off that came from a police constable. The constable, whose name has been withheld on request, was under suspension after being accused of murdering a gangster. However, the constable was still in touch with his informants. In fact, after being suspended and branded a murderer, he had tripled his efforts to get good tip offs which he kept passing on to his seniors in the force to convince them that he was a good cop.

One such tip off came from a foot soldier in the red sanders (a type of sandalwood) mafia. Found in abundance in India, red sanders is in extremely high demand in countries like China and Japan for multiple uses. While it is used in traditional Asian medicine, the wealthy also buy furniture made from red sanders. The soaring demand for red sanders brought its very existence in the country under the threat of extinction. Thus, it was brought under the ambit of the Washington Convention which meant that exporting red sanders now required a certificate.

Like any controlled substance, red sanders became a valuable commodity in the black market. Those who were already involved in the smuggling of gold, silver and electronics now added red sanders to the list.

By this time, a new racket had taken shape. Containers shipped out of the country via the JNPT in Nhava Sheva would often have contraband hidden inside one of the many cartons in the consignment. The entire racket first operated purely on blind luck, with smugglers hoping that the contraband would not be noticed in the random checks conducted by customs officers. Later, the racket flourished because of corruption. Smuggling gangs made their own contacts in the customs department and paid them handsomely for clearing their containers at the docks, just as they were earlier paid to stay away from landing points in the city.

The biggest such case in recent history was that of the serial blasts of March 1993. Dawood Phanse, the landing agent for the D-gang, smuggled AK-56 assault rifles, RDX and hand grenades into the country by filling the pockets of customs officers to their brim. In fact, senior customs officer, S.N. Thapa and several others were accused in the bomb blast case for their alleged connivance in the smuggling of RDX, grenades and guns.

In order to make detection difficult for the law enforcement, red sanders which is usually found in states like Andhra Pradesh, Karnataka and Tamil Nadu is first brought by road to Mumbai through long winding routes. Hidden under other goods like garments or cotton, the truck carrying it changes drivers several times before reaching Mumbai. Then, the cartons are loaded into containers and shipped off to their destinations.

The suspended constable received a tip off that a large consignment of red sanders was going to be smuggled out of the country. The constable slipped his informant a few more 1000-rupee notes (demonetization was still a dozen years away and 1000 rupee notes were still in circulation) and the person told him that the consignment, which was packed and waiting, was currently in trucks parked in the Sewri area.

The constable knew that the Mumbai crime branch was at its peak of omnipotence in those days and that Sharma was among the most popular encounter specialist at the branch. He knew that passing on a solid tip to Sharma would earn him a place in his good books and might strengthen the constable's prospects of getting his name cleared and retrieving his job. The constable told Sharma what he had learned and assured him that it was a good tip.

'I am already suspended, sir,' he said, unconsciously standing at attention in front of his superior. 'I stand to gain nothing by wasting your time.'

Finally, Sharma nodded and put together a team and descended on the spot where the trucks were parked. The vehicles were being guarded by a few thugs who were obviously low-level lieutenants for an organized crime syndicate. Sharma rounded them all up and dragged them to the lock up. One of them, who was still wet behind the ears, started singing like a canary after being subjected to the police's special interrogation techniques. His confession yielded two results. Firstly, another truck full of red sanders was seized. Secondly, the crime branch got the details of the consignment.

Sharma sent a team to JNPT to get the details of the consignment. He found that the consignment was signed by one Mukund Patel. Sharma smiled at the breakthrough. He had hit the pay dirt. Patel was a known associate of the Chhota Rajan gang and his involvement in the consignment reeked of a bigger scam. Since the time Rajan had parted ways with his former boss—Dawood Ibrahim Kaskar—and started his own gang, he was running operations from Bangkok in Thailand.

Once again, Sharma laid out a dragnet and picked up Patel within a week. Patel maintained that he knew nothing about the red sanders consignment despite the paperwork bearing his name as the clearing agent. Since Patel could be hiding some juicy information, Sharma decided to use a different approach.

Patel was officially placed under arrest and remanded to police custody. Sharma knew that Patel had access to a battery of lawyers and that third-degree torture, and other such methods might boomerang on him with complaints in the court and human rights commission. Sharma had to outwit Patel without letting him know that he was being played. For the next few days, Sharma ridiculed the hell out of Patel.

'Look at the gang you work for,' Sharma scoffed at Patel. 'They are involved in such huge activities not just in India but also abroad. Your bhai sits in Bangkok and rules here as well as there. All those who matter to him get important jobs. And you? *Tu kya kar raha hai*? *Chandan ka* smuggling? (What are you doing? Smuggling sandalwood?)'

As the days passed, Patel's frustration grew. Sharma kept dropping names of other known gang members and goading Patel about how they were all big shots in the hierarchy while Patel himself had gotten nowhere. Tired of the mockery and the constant taunts when in fact he was quite high up in Rajan's syndicate, he finally cracked.

'Say what you will,' Patel told Sharma. 'But I am pretty important in the gang.'

'*Jaa bey*!' Sharma replied. 'Important people don't get stuck in seedy rackets.'

'This? This is just one of the things I know,' Patel said. 'I know more, a lot more...'

Sharma just made a sceptical face and looked away, making a dismissive gesture with his hand.

'You don't believe me? Weapons! Guns have landed in the country, boss!' Patel blurted in a boastful manner. 'And you guys are sitting here and teasing me like school children.'

Struggling to keep his face deadpan, Sharma turned to Patel. 'What the fuck. Do you have proof?'

'Proof?' Patel snorted. 'I am the proof! I saw everything with my own eyes!'

The trick employed by Sharma is known as *chaabi lagaana* in Hindi and is a widely used interrogation technique. Simply put, it means winding the key of a toy monkey (here the subject of interrogation) till it starts jumping.

And as the key turned, Patel spilled the entire story. Just a month ago, he had gone to Bangkok and met Rajan. Over a sumptuous meal that he had with his boss—yes, he shared a meal with Rajan because he was no small fry—he saw with his own eyes as Santosh Shetty, top Rajan aide, packed modern, imported weapons and ammunition into plastic bags and sealed them. The packets were then concealed in drums of grease to avoid detection. Thus, a container full of grease drums could easily have a few drums carrying weapons hidden in them. Patel's job was to make sure the weapons entered India without any trouble. He told Rajan to not worry. He was, after all, Mukund Patel.

The more Sharma expressed his scepticism, the more details came tumbling out. There were over thirty guns, Patel claimed, manufactured by reputed gun-makers including Wembley and Scott, Smith and Wesson and Colt. They were purchased from the top gunrunners in Thailand along with hundreds of rounds of ammunition.

Even as Patel was talking, one of Sharma's officers dialled the JNPT docks. A container of grease had indeed come from Bangkok around a week ago and was waiting to be picked up. It had been sent in the name of a Mumbai based company. In just an hour, Sharma's team confirmed that the company was a shell company—a front that exists only on paper. Back in the Unit VII lock up, Patel was still talking nonstop, trying to prove how well-connected and indispensable he was to the Rajan gang.

'*Kya planning hai bol nahin sakta!* (I can't tell you how great the planning was!)' Patel boasted. 'They even had a dry run. Shetty sent a consignment containing barrels of grease from Bangkok to JNPT around two weeks earlier to see if there were any hitches in the process. There were none.'

Sharma grabbed Patel by his shirt collar, dragged him close and breathed in his face. 'Give me the bloody consignment number,' he snarled.

Patel was stunned at Sharma's instantaneous transformation. The officer who only a few minutes ago was disinterested in his loose talk was suddenly dangerously all business. A terrified Patel blurted out the consignment number. Minutes later, a police Gypsy zoomed out of the Unit VII compound in Bandra and made a screaming turn onto Hill Road. Nhava Sheva was still a couple of hours away. Sharma did not want some hidden hands to move the consignment.

And when Sharma reached the docks, he was totally speechless. Barrel after barrel was opened. True enough, the crime branch recovered a total of thirty-eight guns from the barrels and close to 1000 rounds of ammunition.

Rajan, as part of his war against the D-gang, had sent the guns to be distributed among his foot soldiers in Mumbai with orders to decimate Dawood's men in the city. This included everyone from henchmen to financiers. And in every such war, innocent blood is always spilled as collateral damage.

Sharma shuddered to think of the consequences had the guns reached their intended recipients. Pre-emption of a full-scale gang war on the streets was the reason that the Mumbai Police had issued the shoot-to-kill orders in the first place. The arms seize boosted Sharma's popularity to new heights in the police force as well as in the news media.

Police commissioner A.N. Roy addressed a huge press conference to commend the stellar work that 'his boys' had done. Print and television media also played the news tirelessly. This was also dubbed as Roy's biggest success during his stint as the police commissioner of Mumbai.

Sharma was on cloud nine. The commissioner of police now broke the chain of command by ignoring his joint commissioner crime, his DCP and other top brass and he directly called

Sharma to confer with him on several aspects of the investigation and prosecution. In fact, Roy and Sharma were photographed in the same frame by several print media photographers and television journalists. Roy's photographs were splashed in all the newspapers for days on end.

Sharma had won laurels for his investigation, but he had also added several more names to the list of his enemies. The arms seize remained a topic of discussion for a long time. Sharma's seniors congratulated him on preventing another bloodbath in the city. Only Sharma knew that the case had been a terribly low hanging fruit for him.

23

The Witch Hunt and Waterloo

Sharma's phone was ringing off the hook and for all the wrong reasons.

'*Kya hua*, Pradeep? What am I hearing?' a senior officer with whom Sharma had worked earlier asked. This was the seventh such call in a row.

'It's not true, sir. I wasn't even there,' Sharma said, massaging his forehead with his other hand.

'Then why is there a FIR? Why is your name in it?'

'Sir, if I was involved in the encounter, would I not have included my name in the team? Forget that. If I were that kind of a cop and simply wanted a share of the credit, do you think anyone would have refused to include my name? Lakhan was a big target, after all? It's not like I knew beforehand that things would go wrong!'

Four hours ago, a FIR had been registered with the Versova Police Station. The FIR claimed that Ramnarayan Gupta alias Lakhan Bhaiya had been killed in a fake encounter by a team attached to the D.N. Nagar police station outside Nana Nani Park in Versova. Among the sixteen policemen named in the

FIR, the last was Sharma. The FIR had mentioned Section 302, deliberate murder, against all the officers listed.

Lakhan Bhaiya had been on the police's most wanted list for several years. A top lieutenant of the Chhota Rajan gang, Lakhan was said to be number three in the hierarchy, with only Rohit Verma and Rajan over him. Even Ravi Mallesh Bora alias D.K. Rao, a prominent Rajan gang member, reported to Lakhan.

After every encounter, the concerned police team is required by law to register a FIR against the dead gangster, saying that he tried to kill them and was killed when the police returned fire. Over the years, the story of gangsters being killed in 'return-fire' became so common that the news media had a template for news reports, where only the names of the gangsters and police officers would be changed and a quote or two added for the sake of variety.

The official version of the events of 11 November 2006, as recorded by the D.N. Nagar police team in their complaint, goes like this. Police Inspector Pradeep Suryavanshi received information from 'reliable informants' that Lakhan would be visiting the Versova area that same evening. Suryavanshi, popularly known as 'Nana' in his circle, assembled a team and laid a trap at Nana Nani Park where the informant had claimed Lakhan would be. As soon as he was seen coming, the cops approached him, identified themselves and asked them to surrender. Instead, he whipped out a weapon tucked in his trousers and shot at the police team and was thus killed in the 'return-fire'.

However, the version detailed by Lakhan's brother, lawyer Ramprasad Gupta, in a complaint that he submitted to the office of the Commissioner of Police, Mumbai, on 14 November was different. According to Gupta, his brother, along with another man, Anil Bheda, were picked up from Vashi by a team of policemen in plainclothes early on the morning of 11 November. Both were illegally detained by the police and in the evening, Suryavanshi and his team bundled Lakhan into a vehicle, took him to Nana Nani Park and shot him at an opportune moment when there were no eyewitnesses. The police later let Bheda go, after putting the fear of God into him. After returning home, Bheda told his wife that he had gone to Shirdi because he suddenly felt like getting '*Baba ka ashirvad* (the saint's blessings).'

When Gupta first submitted the letter, nobody was particularly worried. Definitely not Sharma and for good reason. On the morning that the police team was alleged to have picked up Lakhan from Vashi, Sharma was on duty at the police station. He had even made an entry in the station diary saying he had supervised the morning parade. All police stations hold a parade every morning and evening, where the Senior Inspector or the Police Inspector (Crime) brief the personnel before they start their shift. Even the team that had conducted the encounter were not worried.

Meanwhile, Gupta filed a writ petition seeking an inquiry into his brother's death. After over a year of hearings and reports, on 10 October 2007, the Bombay High Court directed the Mumbai Police to start a probe into the matter. A Special Investigation Team was set up under DCP K.M.M. Prasanna, who was then in charge of Zone IX—the Bandra to Andheri belt—and periodic reports were submitted to the High Court.

The policemen who conducted the encounter landed in the dock for two main reasons. The first was that immediately after Lakhan and Bheda were picked up from Vashi, a shopkeeper who knew Lakhan well called Gupta and told him about it. Gupta tried to find Lakhan himself and when that failed, he shot off a series of telegrams and faxes. Three telegrams were sent to the offices of the police commissioners of Mumbai, Thane and Navi Mumbai at 4.08 p.m., while two more were sent to the offices of the Maharashtra chief minister and a DCP level officer in Mumbai at 6.28 p.m. Gupta also sent faxes to the Thane and Navi Mumbai commissioner's offices at 4.45 p.m. All the messages specified that Lakhan had been picked up in the morning by plainclothes policemen. When the police team, in its report, claimed that Lakhan was shot down after he reached Versova at 8.10 p.m., the discrepancies worked in Gupta's favour.

The second factor was Anil Bheda—the crucial prime witness. After being released on 12 November 2007, Bheda went on to record his statement with the SIT in which he said that he had been picked up and held overnight at the D.N. Nagar lock up, while Suryavanshi's team conducted the fake encounter, and then he was released the next day after being threatened.

Until then, Sharma was leading a carefree life but slowly and stealthily, Sharma's world began to crumble. The cruel wheels of fate had begun to turn in a ruthless manner.

Earlier, in February 2007, Sharma was summarily shunted to Amravati under the pretext that he had served for a long time and Mumbai and not posted in mofussil region. As a rule, officers are supposed to serve in other districts apart from Mumbai, which he had not done. Sharma suspected that the seemingly innocuous transfer to Amravati was part of a larger game plan to clip his wings. Sharma decided to rebel against the transfer and refused to report to duty under the guise of sick leave. The weeks became months and Sharma did not resume work.

Meanwhile, Hemant Karkare, who had freshly been repatriated to his home cadre of Maharashtra after a successful stint at RAW, took charge of the Anti-Terror Squad (ATS). Karkare, who had already immensely benefitted due to Sharma's skills in the IC 814 hijack case, felt that an invaluable asset was being wasted. Karkare mediated on Sharma's behalf, persuading him to return to work. The administration reluctantly gave in to Karkare's pleas. Sharma was posted in the central control room at police headquarters. Sharma was reduced to hearing calls of eve teasing, tree falling, accidents on the highway and such other petty incidents. Sharma put up a brave face against the downgrade. 'Nuclear energy is used to light a *beedi* (hand-rolled cigarette) at the *paanwala*'s shop,' his friends often joked about his plight. Eventually Sharma was transferred to Dharavi Police Station.

In June 2008, when theatres in Thane and Vashi were bombed by Hindu religious groups, Karkare arrested the workers of the right-wing organization, Sanathan Sanstha, and exposed the handiwork of saffron terror in the country. Not many knew that Sharma had provided Karkare valuable assistance in busting the terror module.

It is said that one should avoid making enemies because sometimes one enemy can tilt the balance against the might of a thousand friends. In Sharma's case, that was always waiting to happen. His devil-may-care attitude soon ran out of luck and he learnt the truth in a hard way.

On 30 August 2008, when Sharma returned home, he was shocked to receive a notice from DGP Anami Roy's office which stated that Sharma was dismissed under Article 311 sub section 2 of the Indian Constitution for his alleged nexus with the Mumbai underworld. The article empowers an officer of the rank of the commissioner of police of a city to summarily dismiss a corrupt officer or policemen.

Sharma could not believe his eyes. After twenty-five years of service and fighting organized crime where he had to cultivate sources and informants from the underworld to build cases against mafia, he had never been accused of having links with them. Now, suddenly, the administration found it a compelling reason to sack him on the same grounds for which he was highly appreciated in the recent past.

In fact, Anami Roy himself had lauded Sharma for the arms seize from a container of grease drums at JNPT port in Nhava Sheva. Sharma could bust it only because he had his moles in the underworld. Sharma's assets were now his biggest liability.

'My dismissal was a subject of convenience. Till the time I served a purpose, I was useful to them. When they realized I had become inconvenient they sacked me. Just because they felt I was expendable,' Sharma said.

But there was more in store for him.

DCP K.M. Prasanna's SIT, which was probing the investigation, suddenly went off track and became Sharma-centric. Whatever the case, on 20 September 2009, after three long years after the encounter incident, the SIT led by Prasanna registered an FIR with the Versova police against all the cops named in the encounter, including Sharma who was the sixteenth and the last accused named in the FIR.

That was the most shocking revelation. The nugget of information was made viral in a systematic manner. When he first heard the news, Sharma thought it was a practical joke. As the media got whiff of it and his phone started ringing, he called an officer he knew in Versova simply to make sure there wasn't some misunderstanding. Unfortunately for him, there wasn't.

He was officially an accused in a murder case.

Sharma was totally incredulous at the news. He was a veteran of over 111 encounters. Some of the encounters had been highly controversial which tried to put him in the dock and had the media and human rights activists baying for his blood for months. But till now no FIR or court cases had been registered against him. And he had not even been present at this encounter.

Sharma had a sinking feeling that this FIR was far too motivated. There was a greater design at play here. Sharma understood that the probe against others in the police team was merely ornamental and he was the epicentre of the raging storm. This might very well become his Waterloo.

As per the law, despite a registration of FIR, the investigation officer is not under compulsion to arrest the persons named in the case. It is solely the prerogative of the officer to make the arrest or not. But in Sharma's case this prerogative was exercised diligently. Despite being the last one to be named in the FIR, he was arrested first, much before the others.

This was done despite the Maharashtra Administrative Tribunal's (MAT) overturning of the state chief, Anami Roy's, order of Sharma's dismissal. Sharma, as per the Tribunal's order, was due to be reinstated on 10 January 2010.[7] He was arrested a day before the court order.

Something was definitely fishy about the whole business.

---

[7] DGP/11/22/P.R.S./30.08.2008, Director General of Police, Maharashtra State, Mumbai. Order of dismissal from service under Proviso (b) to sub clause (2) of Article 311 of the Constitution of India.

24

Salaskar's Martyrdom

Sharma stared at the television for a long time. His eyes were fixated at the ticker at the bottom of the screen which repeatedly displayed the breaking news of the moment. His heart filled with sorrow. Tears welled in his eyes, streaming down his cheeks.

'*Bulaya kyon nahin?* (Why did not you call?)' Sharma muttered to himself. '*Saath mein milkar maarte* (We would have fought together).'

On the night of 26 November 2008, Salaskar rang the doorbell of his home in Goregaon. He was returning early from work, a rare occasion. He had never hesitated to sacrifice his personal life for his duties. Divya, his twenty-one-year-old daughter, could not resist asking him jovially why he had come home early. Salaskar replied that he merely wanted to surprise her. Under the hard casing of a cop who had nearly eighty encounters to his name, Vijay Salaskar was a regular man who deeply loved his family and, most importantly, his daughter.

Salaskar heard the clanging of utensils in the kitchen. Smita, his wife, had cooked a special dish for him. He had great admiration for the efficiency with which she'd managed the household and the family while he fought criminals on the streets of Mumbai. He often spoke about wanting to spend more time with her.

'Now that you're early for once, let us go out for a long drive,' Divya told her father.

Salaskar nodded. Time had passed rather quickly. The little baby girl whom he would often carry on his back playfully had grown up. Smita emerged from the kitchen with a plate and a bowl and arranged it neatly on the dinner table.

'Let your father eat first,' she said smilingly. 'And then you can go.'

Salaskar looked at Smita. Like any other married couple, they had been through the crests and troughs of living together. Salaskar's devotion to his duty was the primary cause of friction between the two. He had prioritized his work so much that he'd stopped having dinner at home. Most of the time, he ate outside with his colleagues or his informants. Salaskar regularly missed anniversaries and dismissed such events as insignificant. This irked Smita who would sulk and not talk to him for days. His absence from the house on account of work had grown to such proportions that Smita had often confronted him if he was having an affair. At this accusation, Salaskar—one of the toughest cops in Mumbai—would try to woo his wife with a delectable dose of romance. 'My dear Smita, after you I only love my own *asmita* (self-respect),' he would say. 'Everything else is immaterial.'

However, Smita never fell for it. But today was a rare instance when Salaskar had come home for dinner. He had started making some effort to balance his work and family life. He folded his sleeves and eased into the chair. A timely dinner was also a rarity in his profession. Despite his superstar status in the force, he had never shied away from regular duties like nakabandi when ordered and had often gone hungry. His wife served him the curry and poured him a glass of water.

'We'll go after you finish dinner,' Divya said and made her way towards her room. 'I'll be waiting, okay?'

Salaskar smiled and nodded again. He was a doting father to his child. Finally, he would get the chance to bond with his daughter. He looked forward to the moment as he began eating under Smita's watchful eyes. Smita was waiting for her husband to approve her cooking and broaden his eyebrows in appreciation. Salaskar savoured the tasteful curry but did not shower her with praises.

'More?' Smita asked, prodding for some approval.

Salaskar's phone rang before he could answer. A call from the Crime Branch meant important business. He wiped the tips of his fingers and answered. As he took in the magnitude of the news, his wife only saw her husband's ice-cold face that gave nothing away. The conversation barely lasted a minute. Salaskar disconnected the call and washed his hands clean.

'I have to go,' he said to his wife. 'There's talk of some attack.'

'Attack?'

Salaskar did not have the time to elaborate. He rang his subordinates and ordered them to meet him at designated spots so that he could pick them up. Then, he wore his shoes and checked his weapon. Within minutes, he was out of the door. Divya emerged out of her room wondering what was taking her father so long. She was getting impatient for the drive. Instead, she only saw an empty chair and understood that her father had been abruptly called for duty again. Her only refrain was that he hadn't wished her goodbye when he left the house that night.

Later, Smita and Divya turned on the television to find out that Mumbai was under a terrorist attack. Gunfire was being reported from multiple spots in the city. When most people were rushing as far away as they could get from south Mumbai, Vijay Salaskar was driving towards the battle-zone to smoke out the terrorists. Visuals started streaming on the television. At 11.30 p.m. the TV showed fumes of fire billowing from the dome of the Taj Mahal Hotel at Colaba. Smita panicked for her husband's safety.

To reassure her mother, Divya called 'Superman' on her phone. It was the moniker under which she had saved her father's number. It was a shift in her perception. As a teenager, she had saved the same number as 'Control Room', a joke that Salaskar had shared with his close colleagues while commenting on the mischievously bubbly nature of his daughter. Much to Divya's surprise, her Superman answered her phone.

'Where are you?' she asked.

'I am at the spot,' Salaskar whispered back.

The gigantic, roman numeral clock atop the Chhatrapati Shivaji Terminus (CST) railway station ticked towards midnight. The heritage building had been turned into a graveyard. A pool of dead bodies was strewn in the passenger hall. The Victorian architecture of its pillars was smeared with the blood of innocent Mumbaikars. Outside, the towering structure of the CST, Vijay Salaskar teamed up with ATS Chief Hemant Karkare and Additional Commissioner of Police Ashok Kamte. The three officers were about to launch a manhunt for the two terrorists who had wreaked this mayhem. The terrorists were later identified as Ajmal Kasab and Abu Ismail.

A few hours earlier, around 9.30 pm, Kasab and Ismail had stormed into CST with AK-47 rifles in their hands. Their indiscriminate firing had killed as many as fifty-eight people and injured many more. Hand grenades were thrown at civilian passengers. The carnage lasted for more than an hour. Hemant Karkare had arrived at the spot first. Then, he had donned a bulletproof vest and a helmet and with a handful of constables, he tried to locate the terrorists on platform number one. But by this time, Kasab and Ismail had made their exit towards the Cama and Albless Hospital.

Hemant Karkare, now reinforced with the additional firepower of Kamte and Salaskar, decided to head towards the hospital in pursuit of the terrorists. The team were accompanied by four constables, including constable Arun Jadhav who had been Salaskar's bodyguard for years.

Salaskar was a famed sharpshooter in the Mumbai Police. But he was also a very reliable driver, especially in high pressure situations. This was evident from the many times he had taken responsibility of the wheel during the encounters of Shrikant Mama and the Makadwala brothers. So, Salaskar asked the driver of the Toyota Qualis to get into the backseat.

'I'll drive,' Salaskar said and moved into the driver's seat.

This was the costliest mistake on that night committed by any police officer. A free and alert Salaskar could have been the biggest asset in those moments. Ashok Kamte was armed with an AK-47, however, he had not seen much action. He was seated next to Salaskar. Karkare was in the backseat with his weapon drawn and ready. Arun Jadhav and three other constables were also in the back. A few other guards were left stationed at CST.

Salaskar began driving towards Cama and Albless Hospital which was barely five minutes away from the railway station. He kept an eye out for the terrorists. The vehicle treaded carefully on the deserted road. The wireless in the vehicle cackled to life. An important piece of information was relayed. *The terrorists are hiding behind a red vehicle near Rang Bhavan.*

Salaskar slowed down to a speed below 20 kmph, looking out for a red vehicle in the dark of the night. As they crossed the Crime Branch building, Abu Ismail and Ajmal Kasab emerged from their hiding place and ambushed the police vehicle, firing a hail of bullets from their automatic weapons. Gunfire resounded through the air. Salaskar returned fire but the policemen were confined to the vehicle and thus at a disadvantage. An incessant burst of bullets flew towards him. The windshield began cracking.

From the backseat, Jadhav aimed to fire but the enemy's bullets had pierced through his right hand and left shoulder. He was rendered incapable of retaliatory action. His stengun fell from his hands. He collapsed on the backseat. Other constables dropped dead on top of him. One of the terrorists threw a grenade which missed the target. Salaskar's vision blurred in the cloud of smoke. He was hit. He gasped for breath. In a matter of minutes, Hemant Karkare and Ashok Kamte were dead.

Abu Ismail and Ajmal Kasab menacingly approached the police vehicle. Kasab opened the passenger door and pulled Ashok Kamte's dead body out of the car. Buried under a pile of his colleagues' bodies, Arun Jadhav saw Ajmal Kasab from a distance of a few feet, but his injuries were far too severe for him to take any action.

Ismail opened the door on the driver's side. He pulled out Salaskar, who was ridden with bullets and covered in blood, and dropped him to the ground. Jadhav hoped that Salaskar, his beloved boss, would respond and kill these two bastards just like he had killed so many criminals. But Salaskar was fatally hit. Jadhav had protected his boss for years and Salaskar had trusted Jadhav with his life. Often Jadhav would even stand guard at the door if Salaskar visited the washroom on a regular day of duty. But on 26/11 when Salaskar had been pushed to the verge of death, Jadhav's hands had been completely paralysed by enemy bullets. Jadhav heard the relay on the vehicle's wireless again. Word had reached control room that the police vehicle had come under fire. Other policemen were ordered to approach the white police Qualis with caution.

Kasab pulled out Hemant Karkare's dead body from the middle row of the car. Then, he moved into the passenger's seat in front. Abu Ismail grabbed the steering which was only a few minutes ago in Vijay Salaskar's hands. The two terrorists began driving towards Mantralaya. On the back row, only Arun Jadhav had some amount of life left in his lungs. The other constables were all dead. Worse, Jadhav had to endure the weight of their unmoving bodies. It was the heaviest burden he would ever bear. Jadhav held his breath and played dead to prevent drawing any attention from Kasab or Ismail.

The terrorists sped off in the police vehicle leaving behind a trail of smoke and blood. In the lane near Rang Bhavan, only a few metres away from the Crime Branch office, two top IPS officers of the Mumbai Police had been martyred. But Vijay Salaskar was still putting up a brave fight against death. He shouted out for help in Marathi. His desperate calls could be heard by those who were hiding in the nearby buildings, but no one dared to come to his assistance. He continued to shout. Perhaps, he believed he had a chance if he received timely medical assistance. But it took a while for a police party to arrive at the spot.

Salaskar was rushed to G.T. Hospital where, true to his nature, he continued to fight against the odds. He was bleeding heavily. Yet, he signalled with his eyes for someone to remove a thick bunch of keys in the pockets of his trousers which was hurting him. Though the doctors and paramedics tried their best, Inspector Vijay Salaskar was martyred while protecting his city from Pakistani terrorists.

Perhaps, things could have been different had Salaskar not chosen to drive on that fateful day. Ashok Kamte was an extremely fit and brave police officer. Hemant Karkare had also served with the elite RAW in Austria before taking over the Maharashtra Anti-Terrorism Squad. But neither Kamte nor Karkare had seen the kind of action that Salaskar had been a part of. Salaskar had earned his stripes with Mumbai's elite 'Encounter Squad' and had engaged in gun battles with criminals very frequently in his career. Perhaps, if he had the advantage of a better tactical position, Salaskar would have trumped over the terrorists who eventually killed him. But that was not to be. And thus, a legendary warrior of the Mumbai Police fell in the battlefield.

For the bravery that Inspector Vijay Salaskar displayed while protecting his nation, he was posthumously awarded with India's highest peacetime military decoration—the Ashok Chakra. To this day, his heroic deeds continue to inspire colleagues in the uniform and, the citizens of a grateful country.

Pradeep Sharma, Salaskar's former friend turned rival, had tears in his eyes when he heard of Salaskar falling to the bullets of the terrorists. Over ten years have passed, but Sharma's eyes still moisten whenever Salaskar's name is mentioned. He often reminisces about the pranks he pulled off with Vijay at the academy. Sharma and Salaskar fought many battles together, putting their lives in each other's hands and coming out alive from all those dangerous situations. Sharma deeply regrets not being able to fight alongside Salaskar on the night of 26/11; he had been dismissed a few months ahead of the terrorist attack and was at home on that fateful night. Salaskar would have never thought of seeking his erstwhile friend's help because he was not in service anymore.

'I don't enjoy my successes with as much intensity after Salaskar's exit,' Sharma said in an interview. 'He was my benchmark. The fervour to keep going was because I thought he was watching my accomplishments.'

25

Ustadi Ustade Se

'Get inside, everyone. Come on, get inside!'

'You three, move. Fast.'

'*Abey chal na*! (Move will you!) Are you deaf?'

The guards at Thane Central Jail went about gathering the inmates so that they could be packed off to their cells. Some of the most hardened thugs of the city shot the guards tough looks as they made their way back into the confines of the iron bars. Within minutes, the yards and corridors were devoid of any inmates and only the guards remained. Superintendent Yogesh Desai, who was in charge of the prison, confirmed over the wireless that all prisoners were locked in before giving the next order.

'Bring them,' he said crisply.

A minute later, the door to a separate structure in one corner of the jail was opened. Sharma, followed by six others, walked out and were escorted to the gate by the prison guards. Here, officers and constables from the Local Arms Unit took over, herding them into a waiting vehicle to take them to the court in Mumbai.

Sharma had been lodged in Thane Central Jail for the last six months. Following his arrest, the SIT had not even sought a single day's police custody, and for good reason. Every day that Sharma would spend at the police station lock up was a risk, either for him or for any other inmate who would be unfortunate or just stupid enough to try and start a violent incident. Secondly, there was no need for custodial interrogation. Sharma's arrest in the Lakhan Bhaiya case was based on a statement by Anil Bheda which was false. The SIT knew Sharma was not going to say a word and the longer he remained in police custody, the longer there was a chance of him making an allegation against the investigating officer in court during a remand hearing. Hence, the day after his arrest, when Sharma was produced at the Metropolitan Magistrate's Court in Andheri, he was remanded to judicial custody and sent to Thane Central Jail.

A policeman is wired to acclimatize himself to any situation, even if it is behind bars. Sharma and his co-accused cops, who were soon arrested one after the other, knew that most of the population inside the jail were their enemies. Those who did not have a personal axe to grind might try to strike out at them simply to make a name for themselves.

There is a clearly defined pecking order among prison inmates. If you desire respect, you have to beat a fellow inmate. The bigger the inmate you defeat, the higher the amount of respect you command. In 2013, gangster Abu Salem was attacked by fellow inmate Devendra Jagtap inside Taloja Central Jail. Jagtap, who had managed to smuggle a gun inside the prison, shot at Salem twice, and later told his interrogators that he wanted to make a name for himself. Killing Salem would have granted him instant fame not only inside the prison but outside as well.

The same could be said about Sharma. Any inmate who managed to inflict even a single scratch on his body would be a runaway hero for life. Even if the rest of the police force teamed up and shot him down, his name would forever be engraved in the annals of history as the one who got Sharma.

Desai, an experienced policeman, realized this, and hence every time Sharma was taken either out of the prison or back inside, Desai would lock the entire prison down. The other inmates had become used to this routine by now. Every time there was an out of turn lockdown, they knew Sharma was either going for or returning from a court appearance or a medical check-up at Thane Civil Hospital.

Perhaps, it was because of this threat that the prison authorities did not object too strongly to Sharma's prolonged stay at the hospital. Of the three and a half years he spent in judicial custody, two and a half years were at Thane Civil Hospital's prison ward. Everyone concerned was comfortable with Sharma being safe and sound in a hospital rather than at constant risk inside the prison.

As the police van made its way to court, Sharma turned to face the window. It was the only time he got a glimpse of the world outside the prison walls and every time Sharma would hungrily soak it in. The buildings, familiar police stations and chowkies, the billboards, the maddening Mumbai traffic, the bells of temples or churches, the azans of mosques, the honking of horns and even the odd loudspeaker at the occasional wedding brought along unfathomable comfort.

The court appearance was short; the judicial custody period was extended to a later date. But Sharma had more important things on his mind that day. As he exited the courtroom, a policeman with the Modus Operandi Bureau (MOB) of the Mumbai Crime Branch fell into step beside him.

'You needed me?' the policeman asked.

Even though he was technically a jailbird, Sharma's network was still active. He utilized his court and hospital visits to keep abreast of what was happening in the underworld as well as within the police force, thanks to his colleagues and friends who always came to meet him at court.

'Get me a picture of Vicky Malhotra,' Sharma said in a soft voice without turning towards the MOB officer. 'And his dossier.'

The demand was a well thought out one. Within two months of his stint at jail, Sharma had learned that Rajan, who had recovered from his injuries following the attack on him in 2000, was back in business and was gunning for him. He had sent word to Malhotra, one of his closest aides, that he wanted Sharma dead. The news didn't scare Sharma, but it certainly got him thinking. For Malhotra, who had always enjoyed a position of power in Rajan's gang, killing Sharma was a matter of prestige. He would do whatever he could in order to please his master as well as to etch his name in history. More importantly, Malhotra was also lodged at the Thane jail and would have a lot of opportunities to do so, S.P. Desai's precautions notwithstanding.

Over the next several court appearances, Sharma, through his network, slowly obtained all information about the contract on his name. He was somewhat disappointed when he learned that Malhotra's reward was going to be a measly Rs 5 lakh, an amount which was already paid to Malhotra's aide and was being held in escrow. Within a month, he knew exactly who arranged for the money, who was holding it and who was acting as a go-between for Malhotra and Rajan.

Then, he put his plan into motion. The first step was to ask the MOB officer for Vicky Malhotra's picture. Criminal gangs and police departments are the most porous when it comes to keeping a secret. Just as Sharma learned about the hit sanctioned by Rajan, Malhotra was bound to know that Sharma had asked for his photograph. Sharma knew that Malhotra was in touch with some officers with the Crime Branch and passed on the occasional titbit of information to them, in exchange for similar favours. He was, in fact, counting on word reaching Malhotra.

Meanwhile, Malhotra, who was getting increasingly frustrated, tried his best to get close to Sharma but in vain. Desai's precautions protected Sharma in prison, and at court, Sharma was surrounded by a tight security cordon as well as his own friends, some of them policemen who were always armed. Malhotra kept trying even after he got bail in 2010 but to no avail.

Finally, a month after he got bail, he learned that Sharma had sought information about him from the MOB. A terrified Malhotra understood that Sharma knew about his attempts to kill him and convinced himself that this was his death knell. He frantically called a Mumbai Crime Branch officer that he was in touch with and begged the cop to arrange a meeting with Sharma. For three whole weeks, the officer tried to get in touch with Sharma, who knew exactly what was happening and pointedly ignored the officer.

Finally, a desperate Malhotra lay in wait across the street from a back gate at Thane Central Jail, which he knew was used to bring Sharma in and out of the prison. When he saw Sharma alight from the police van after a court appearance, he went running to him.

As was his habit, Sharma stood outside the compound for a few minutes, talking to his friends, a courtesy allowed to him by the guards. Just as he was turning away to enter the prison compound, Malhotra came up to him, sweating.

'*Salaam sahab*,' he said, bowing down and touching Sharma's feet.

Sharma kept his face stony and just looked at Malhotra, letting him sweat.

'*Nahi, aise hi ... socha salaam kar lu* (No, just thought I'd greet you),' Malhotra stammered. 'Just wanted to meet you, sir.'

Sharma only nodded.

'I'm Vicky, saab. Vicky Malhotra,' he went on, offering his hand.

Sharma did not move. '*Bol* (Speak).'

'No, no. Nothing.' Vicky's hand, after a few seconds, slowly dropped to his side. 'Just ... you know ... I hope you are being careful, sahab. *Bahot log peeche padey hain na aapke* (Too many people are after your life, sir).'

Sharma looked Malhotra straight in the eye. '*Kaun kiske peeche pada hai, mujhko sab maloom hai* (I know who is after whose life),' he said and sharply turned around to walk into the prison compound.

Malhotra stood there, unsure if he should be relieved that Sharma had decided to spare him or if their battle was only delayed. Malhotra jumped bail the same year. News reports after Rajan's arrest in 2015 suggested that he might be taking over Rajan's business. But if Vicky was out and at large, Sharma was also back in service by then and on the prowl again.

26

Baba Behind Bars

Sharma was feeling uneasy.

He was sitting in the front passenger seat of his friend's private vehicle and was on his way to Thane Civil Hospital for a medical check-up. His friend was at the wheel and was driving at a moderate speed. Yet, every time he took a turn, or every time another vehicle passed in front of them, Sharma would hold on to the hand hold above and ask his friend to slow down.

It was only by the end of the trip, when the vehicle pulled into the hospital's parking lot, did Sharma understand his apprehension. Sharma was leaving the prison compound after three whole months. After ninety days of only walking around and sitting, the car ride was making him motion sick.

This was only one of the radical changes that Sharma underwent after his arrest on 8 January 2010. Following his arrest, he was produced at the Metropolitan Magistrate's Court in Andheri and remanded to police custody for eight days. He spent the eight days in a separate lock up on the first floor of the police station where he either read newspapers or books or pondered on his fate. Deep down, he knew he was going to win this battle as well. Still, being arrested like a common criminal and spending day behind bars was more depressing than he had imagined.

On 15 January, he was once again produced in court and remanded to judicial custody. The magistrate sent him to Thane Central jail. Sharma reached late at night. Since most of the prison inmates would have an axe to grind, the Superintendent at the prison, Yogesh Desai, had made arrangements beforehand.

Sharma was taken to a separate barrack reserved for death row convicts, who are kept in isolation in their final days. The barrack was secluded and located at a good distance from the other barracks, and was surrounded by its own compound wall, ensuring total security. Usually this was meant to keep the death row convicts inside, however, this time it served the purpose of keeping the other inmates out.

Sharma had already received the court's permission to have home-cooked food delivered to him. Desai was doing everything he could to ensure Sharma's security as well. But life was going to be far from comfortable.

Over the next couple of months, several other accused in the Lakhan Bhaiya encounter case joined Sharma in the barracks. Sharma nursed a deep grudge against the entire team that had conducted the encounter because he had been thrown to the wolves because of their actions. But he also knew that it was pointless. More importantly, it was crucial that they all act in solidarity because it was them against the world now.

A month later, an IPS officer who was posted with the prisons department at the time visited the Thane jail for a supposedly routine inspection. He entered Sharma's barracks and started lambasting him about giving the police force a bad name.

All eyes turned to Sharma as he drew himself up to his full height.

'Me? I gave the force a bad name? I've been thrown in here in a cooked-up case. And what is the charge against me? Rape? Murder? Corruption? Even if I did what they say I did, I killed a bloody criminal, something I have always done to keep the city safe. You turn on me, a fellow policeman, in my time of crisis and say I am the one giving the force a bad name?'

The barrack went deathly silent as everyone waited for the senior officer's response. The officer took a long hard look at Sharma and then turned on his heel and walked out. The battle was won. But the war wasn't over.

The same officer took it upon himself to make things difficult for Sharma when he was admitted to Thane Civil Hospital frequently over the next three-and-a-half years for various health ailments, including blood pressure, knee joint problems and piles. Sharma spent nearly two years of his imprisonment in the prisoner ward of the hospital, amid questions raised by the SIT and the press about preferential treatment being given to him. All this while, however, Dr Rokde, the surgeon at the hospital, and S.P. Yogesh Desai, submitted timely reports in the court certifying why his stay in the hospital was necessary.

During Sharma's fourth or fifth visit, the officer sent his orderly to meet Sharma with a proposal. He offered to not create any issues in exchange for a favour. The favour was that Sharma had to facilitate the officer's transfer out of the prisons department to other, more lucrative postings. The officer's posting of choice was Navi Mumbai.

Sharma made no promises but sent one of his friends to meet senior officials in the state home department to see what could be done. However, the request fell flat as tales of the officer's corrupt nature had already reached the corridors of the Mantralaya.

'All hell will break loose if I give him a Navi Mumbai posting,' R.R. Patil reportedly said while turning down the request.

The officer then started making fresh demands, which included getting him a flat in Thane at lower rates than the usual or ten acres of land in the Thane district. Sharma turned down both demands and told the officer's orderly that he was done entertaining his nonsense.

The next blow came shortly thereafter, when the SIT probing the case obtained the court's permission to move him and his fellow accused to Nashik Central Jail for 'security reasons'. The objective was to put him in a strange place where he had few friends. Sharma immediately appealed against the order at the High Court. However, till the appeal was heard, he had to go to Nashik.

A convoy of vehicles left from Thane Central Jail, with a vehicle attached to the Thane police acting as the pilot vehicle. All along the way, the pilots were replaced by police vehicles from the concerned jurisdiction. This went on all the way till Nashik.

Throughout the journey, Pradeep Suryavanshi, who had also been arrested and remanded to judicial custody, kept requesting the drivers to stop as he was a diabetic patient and needed to use the toilet. The driver, however, flatly refused saying he had strict orders to not stop for any reason. It was only after repeated entreaties that the convoy stopped once close to Nashik and only for five minutes while Suryavanshi used the toilet.

If Sharma thought the journey was difficult, he had no idea what was in store for him at the prison. It was late night when the party reached the prison, and as no food would be available at the time, Sharma and his co-accused had packed food with them. They stopped just before reaching the prison compound so that they could all have dinner. However, five minutes into the meal, the prison DIG, a female officer, stormed out in full uniform. She was obviously waiting for them. She ordered that the meal be stopped, and all the prisoners be taken to their cells immediately. Repeated requests were made, asking her for five more minutes, as many of the prisoners were on medication and needed to eat before they could take their pills. All the pleas, however, fell on deaf ears and the prisoners went to sleep half-hungry.

During the fifteen days that Sharma and the others spent in Nashik jail, as an added insult, they were made to wear prisoners' uniforms, a practice that is reserved for convicts not undertrials. Finally, the High Court dismissed the transfer order on the grounds that the Nashik jail houses convicts, while only undertrials are lodged in Thane, and that Sharma would be safer in Thane.[8]

The humiliation wasn't the only battle that Sharma had to fight. Time and again, during his hospital stays, Sharma was informed through his network that Chhota Rajan had put out a hit on his head, and that several hitmen were trying to kill him. Vicky Malhotra was just one such gang member who had been given the task. Rajan, unwilling to rely only on one person, had also asked others to try and eliminate Sharma.

Sharma used his time in the hospital to stay fully abreast of developments in the underworld and made sure he was well protected.

---

[8] 1999 (4) BomCR 608

He was unwilling to rely only on the four guards who were posted in the hospital for his protection. Every time he was admitted to the hospital, his friends, both policemen and civilian, would station themselves all around. Some would be in their vehicles watching the hospital from across the street. Others would be in the lobby watching the entrances. Yet others would be with him, keeping an eye on the door.

The cat-and-mouse game went on till 5 July 2013 when the trial court cleared Sharma off all charges.[9]

While it was a glorious day for Sharma, it was also a very painful one. Silently, he stood in the dock as the judge pronounced the order. He was let off while everyone else was found guilty.

Right next to him, Sandeep Sardar, a constable, was sniffing silently. As he was pronounced guilty for the final charge against him, his wife broke down and started crying audibly. The couple had been married for less than a year.

At the same time, Sharma was feeling vindicated. The officers from the SIT watched expressionlessly as the judge ruled that there was not an iota of evidence to prove that he was part of the encounter or had even known about it. One by one, the judge tore through the prosecution, pointing out that Sharma's weapon had been taken for ballistic testing long after he had surrendered it to the armoury, that there was no proof of the fact that Sharma was physically present at the scene of the crime based on cellular location mapping, and that the whole case against him was based on inference of guilt and hypothesis.

---

[9] 'Dismissed Police Officer Acquitted in Fake Encounter Case of Chhota Rajan Aide,' PTI, *India Today*, 5 July 2013. https://www.indiatoday.in/india/west/story/dismissed-police-officer-acquitted-in-fake-encounter-case-of-chhota-rajan-aide-169235-2013-07-05.

The worst was finally behind him. But Sharma still could not go home immediately. The judge declared that the quantum of sentencing would be announced at a later date. Sharma only walked out of the prison on 13 July.

This was the first time he was leaving the prison without an armed police escort. He was aware of the fact that he would be exposed and unarmed and so were his friends. The journey from the prison to his house in Andheri was planned in advance. Sharma, after being officially released, was quickly bundled into a friend's bulletproof car, which drove him to his house. Several other cars followed at varying distances.

As he went up to his house, Sharma could not contain his excitement. He had told his family that they were to never come see him in jail. He wanted to spare them the agony of seeing him living like a common criminal and had promised them that he would return home with his head held high.

And he had finally fulfilled that promise.

27

Boosting David to Decimate Goliath

Blades of nearly seventy spades glinted in the afternoon sun as Sharma looked from left to right. He was standing back to back with twenty of his friends, staring certain death in the eye. They were heavily outnumbered. Had he walked into an inescapable trap?

Deep down, a small part of him chuckled. After an entire career of gunning down hardcore killers, one would have thought that he would get some respite while being off the force. And yet, here he was, in Godforsaken Baghpat, surrounded by seventy men armed with spades.

These are not farmers, he thought. Everything about them—the way they were dressed to how the blades glistened, indicating that the spades were brand new, told him only one thing—the men were hired muscle.

This was only the latest in the string of adventures that he had after coming to Baghpat around a month ago. It was a decision based only on one factor: the trust placed in him time and again by Satyapal Singh when they were both serving officers.

On 31 January 2014, Singh, who was then the Mumbai Police Commissioner, put in his papers. He told reporters, who flocked to his office after hearing the news, that there was no particular reason behind his resignation but let it slip that he had political ambitions. When a reporter followed him to his car on his way out and asked what his priorities were now, he answered, 'Nation building and world peace.'

World peace might have been the objective behind his decision to contest the Lok Sabha seat from Baghpat on a BJP ticket shortly after his resignation but the road to achieving it was far from peaceful. Baghpat, an underdeveloped small town in Uttar Pradesh, was one of the eighty Lok Sabha constituencies which borders Meerut and Ghaziabad—two epicentres for active criminal gangs of organized crime.

Besides, Baghpat was the fiefdom of Chaudhary Charan Singh and his son Ajit Singh, who had been ruling it for years. For a rank newcomer to break their hold would require all the four tactics of war—*saam* (advice), *daam* (bribe), *dand* (punishment) and *bhed* (conspiracy). And Singh only knew of one man who was well versed in all four.

Sharma had been acquitted in the Lakhan Bhaiya murder case and had applied for reinstatement when Singh called him. Sharma thought long and hard. He was no longer in the force and had gone through a murder trial and imprisonment before his name was cleared. He wasn't sure he would command the same respect and fear in Baghpat as he might in Mumbai. But then, he thought, *maraa hua haathi bhi sawa laakh ka hota hai* (even a dead elephant fetches a hefty price).

Sharma made his decision and a week later, landed in Meerut with around twenty of his trusted friends and associates, some from Mumbai and others from Agra. He had worked with the people from Mumbai and the ones from Agra were local hoodlums who would act both as the intimidating mechanism as well as muscle, if the need arose.

Sharma approached his objective the way he approached an encounter. The first step was always to gather intelligence about the enemy. With the help of references garnered over the years, Sharma reached out to as many locals as he could. He could not help noticing that Baghpat was grossly underdeveloped. There were no hotels and Sharma and his team stayed in Meerut and travelled back and forth every day. It did not take Sharma long to realize why. The town of Baghpat was still living on promises made by Charan and Ajit Singh.

It both amused and stunned Sharma when he learned that Ajit Singh, who had been elected twice by the people, would only make two appearances in Baghpat every five years. The first visit would be to fill his nomination form, for which he would arrive by helicopter and leave the same way. The second visit would be on the last day of campaigning for the elections, when his men would organize a massive tractor rally, bringing all of Baghpat to a halt. Then, Ajit Singh would address the crowd from a podium. In both his speeches in the last ten years, the content had been the same.

'I am ashamed of myself,' he would say. 'I have come here like a criminal and to beg for your forgiveness. I have failed to solve your problems.' He would sniff back a tear. 'Only last night, *Tau* came to me in a dream and scolded me to no end.'

Tau is the colloquial word for uncle and is also used as a title of respect in north India. Ajit Singh's father, Charan Singh, was known as Tau in Baghpat. Having appealed to the people's emotions, Ajit would then proceed to play with them. He would point to an old man in the crowd, addressing him as Tau.

'*Upar aao, Tau. Nahi aa jao. Idhar aao* (Come on the stage, uncle, come this side),' he would say to the old man with wizened white moustaches, who would slowly come up to the stage, leaning on his *latth* (wooden stick used for walking support). Ajit would them remove his sandal and hand it over to the old man, exhorting him to hit him with it for his crimes. Rumour has it that the old man was a plant.

Sharma knew he had his work cut out for him. But he also realized that the gullibility of the people was something he could work with. After all, he thought, the best manipulator is the best politician.

The next day, Sharma's team fanned out in Baghpat and sought meetings with all the *bahubali*s (big shot thugs) of the village who lent their allegiance to Ajit Singh once every five years for a price. Sharma's friends Googled his name, and let the local strongmen see the results for themselves. For thugs who had seldom stepped outside their little kingdoms, a man who had killed over 100 dreaded criminals and then walked free on a murder charge was someone to take very seriously.

Sharma's team kept up the exercise for two to three weeks and by the end of the period, the fear psychosis had either won the thugs to Sharma's side or discouraged them from supporting those in power.

Next, Sharma approached the sand mining mafia in Baghpat and sought their support. The sand mining mafia are an institution unto themselves and their loyalty was going to be a huge feather in the cap. Over frequent, patient meetings Sharma assured them that they would get all that they needed once Satyapal Singh came to power.

'Look at the place now. And look at Mumbai. He has headed the police force of Mumbai. You think he won't make a difference here? And anything else you need, you have my number,' he assured them.

Not only did everyone connected to the sand mining industry agree to vote for them, they also provided them with vehicles for the rest of their stay in Baghpat.

Ajit Singh wasn't idle during this time. When he first heard that Pradeep Sharma was in his backyard, he could not believe it. He called some of his contacts in Mumbai and one of them, a personal secretary working for a high-ranking politician, got in touch with one of Sharma's former colleagues and asked for Sharma's current number. The cop, however, was more loyal to Sharma than the bureaucrat, and told Sharma about it.

'Give him one of my defunct numbers,' Sharma told him after thanking him. 'Tell him this is the only one you have.'

Now, Sharma knew the enemy was sniffing at his tracks. It was time to get creative. Every night, after the day's work was done, he would go with his team to a hotel in Meerut where they were staying. Half an hour later, he would quietly slip out with one trusted friend from Mumbai in tow, and go to a smaller, less conspicuous hotel, where he would spend the night and come back in the morning.

The tactic paid off when one night, a police team led by the local superintendent conducted a 'raid' on the hotel where Sharma's team was staying. The police found some sample ballot papers and some cash, which every campaigning politician's team is bound to have. While no case was registered, the police did detain the team for nearly a day and leaked every detail to Ajit Singh who, in turn, leaked it to the press. However, the police did not find the one person they had come for—Sharma—and had to return empty handed on that front.

Ajit Singh spared no effort to smear his opponent's name in the local press, and a concerned Satyapal Singh turned to Sharma. His man Friday, however, was not concerned. He hardly had the clout to get the local police to raid Ajit Singh's campaigning offices, but he was already plotting his next move.

Having worked at Chandan Chowky and dealing with Bollywood figures came in handy. Sharma's team succeeded in convincing Sunny Deol to visit Baghpat and appeal to the Jaat electorate. The idea turned out to be a runaway success and over five lakh people turned up to watch their favourite Paaji. The crowd was so out of control that despite a cordon of bodyguards, they still managed to tear Deol's shirt and break the rear-view mirror of his car.

Even as an enraged Deol was on his way back, a group of Ajit Singh plants in the crowd started pelting stones at his convoy. Deol managed to make it out of there without a scratch. But Sharma got his opportunity. Using every form of social media possible, Sharma's team circulated messages blaming Ajit Singh for the stone pelting.

'We Indians regard our guests as our gods. Sunny Deol came here as our guest. Is this how guests will be treated here?' the message said. Overnight, the entire Jaat population had swung in Satyapal Singh's favour.

As time passed, Satyapal Singh started becoming so popular among the locals that his phones were continuously ringing. Half the time, Sharma would speak posing as Singh and assure the callers that all their problems were now Satyapal Singh's responsibility. Sharma started visiting *pradhan*s (local heads) who wielded clout over the villagers. In a few weeks, Sharma had managed to woo and win over 1200 pradhans to his side.

Perhaps, that is why a desperate Ajit Singh tried one last thing to try and scare Sharma away.

On that sunny afternoon, Satyapal Singh, along with Sharma and his team, reached a school which was a polling booth in Baghpat after hearing reports about booth capturing. No sooner had they entered the compound than they were surrounded by seventy to eighty men bearing spades.

Working quickly, Sharma's analytical mind ascertained that these were hired thugs, not farmers. But he also noticed something else. Even though the men were brandishing their weapons, they were hesitating to make a move. *They're afraid*, Sharma thought. All that fear psychosis in the initial few weeks seemed to have paid off. Sharma knew that half the battle is won with the first strike. He was not too keen on harming anyone without enough provocation, but he wasn't exactly going to cower down either.

Slowly, his hand reached towards his waist, where his personal weapon was tucked. At least ten of the seventy thugs followed his hand with their eyes and watched as the gun came up. Sharma could see the sweat break out on their foreheads. Behind him, two of his friends, who were carrying licensed weapons of their own, followed suit and the two constables provided by the police for Singh's protect also raised their service weapons.

For a second, Sharma was back in the force as he yelled, '*Pehle hawa mein maar*! (Fire in the air first!)' The second shot should target their legs and even then, if they do not disperse then fire on their shoulders. This was enough to spread alarm. Sharma's ferocious reputation of killing 111 dreaded gangsters of Mumbai had preceded him.

Four to five guns went off in unison. Half the thugs dropped their spades and started running for their lives. One tried to shuffle forward and Sharma, cocking his head to one side and closing one eye, took direct aim at his forehead. The thugs had seen a picture of Sharma in the same pose back when he was in uniform. The man turned around and ran as hard as he could, followed by the rest of his fellow thugs.

The battle was won. And so was the war.

Satyapal Singh eventually won the Baghpat seat by a margin of 1.5 lakh votes. This was the most humiliating rout for Ajit Singh, a sitting MP for two consecutive elections. He knew that only Sharma could have helped him scale this insurmountable mountain.

28

The Comeback

For the umpteenth time in the day, Pradeep Sharma's phone buzzed. He swiped a finger across the screen and read the message. *Many many hearty congrats, sir. Very happy about the news. See you soon* :)

The number was not a familiar one. But that was hardly surprising as Sharma's phone was flooded with messages, not all of them from known numbers. With a tap of his thumb, Sharma opened the Truecaller app and ran a search for the number. As the name flashed on his screen, he smiled a thin, mirthless smile. He accessed the Options feature and added the number to the blocklist before closing the app. The size of his blocklist had grown significantly in the last few days. People who had chosen to ignore him for years were not missing the slightest excuse to get back in touch now.

The last seven years had not been easy. He had been stripped of his uniform, he had been arrested and paraded before the media like a common criminal and he'd spent three and a half years in jail. It was only after his acquittal in 2013 that he approached the Maharashtra Administrative Tribunal (MAT) seeking reinstatement. Had he not been arrested in January 2010 he would have managed to secure a reinstatement much earlier, but his detention threw a spanner in the works.

Many people wondered why Sharma had chosen to come back to the force. He already had a lucrative security agency, Urban Hawks, in Andheri which took care of his income. Urban Hawks was one of the most sought-after agencies in Mumbai. A charity foundation had also been established in his name. This satisfied his desire to do something for the people around him, a desire that could no longer be fulfilled by policing when he was out of service.

But for Sharma, the uniform had become a part of his soul. It was no longer just a job that he could discard and pick up a new one. It was a calling. This was what he did. This was what he was. It was also important for him to cock a snook at his detractors who presumed that his dismissal and subsequent arrest would be his professional funeral.

Finally, in 2017, the MAT reinstated Sharma as a police inspector with the Maharashtra Police. Within an hour, his cell phone started ringing. If there was one good thing that came out of Sharma's trip to prison and back, it was that he had learned who his true friends were. This included everyone, from policemen, personal contacts, informers and the scores of businessmen whose lives he had saved on more than one occasion.

Even though he had spent seven years away from the job, he still had his ears to the ground. All through his ordeal, he kept getting regular updates from his massive network in Mumbai and the nearby areas. Through the course of his career, he'd made more than a thousand contacts who had supplied him with vital information on the happenings in the gruesome world of crime, and beyond. He knew exactly who was saying what behind his back, who had washed his hands off him, who was going around telling people that they always knew he was a disaster waiting to happen.

And then there were those who had simply disappeared, without so much as a call or a message to enquire about his well-being. Among them were several affluent businessmen who achieved their current status because he was always out there, willing to help every time they got an extortion call. He had pounded the pavement looking for clues, picked up dozens of gang-members to send a strong message to their bosses and on occasion, taken lives of criminals in order to make sure that these businessmen stayed safe. Suddenly, as soon as the handcuffs were clicked around his wrists, all those people had vanished into thin air.

And hence, Sharma was systematically cutting out all the fair-weather friends from his life. Every time one of them sent him a message, he would block their number. Every time someone tried to meet him, he would refuse. Only those who had truly stood by him would get that privilege from now on.

The other effect of Sharma's reinstatement was that a lot of old-time informants who were earlier passing on tip offs to other officers from his batch now gravitated towards him, and not just for selfish reasons.

This was a period when there was a serious vacuum of officers willing to go the extra mile when it came to dealing with the underworld. Praful Bhosale and Ravindra Angre had retired, Vijay Salaskar was no more and those from the encounter era that remained were unwilling to play close to the fire again lest it burn their careers like it had happened, almost, with Sharma.

Anyway, encounters had not been a game for everyone. There were officers who spent their entire careers wriggling out of situations which were likely to end up in encounters because they didn't want even the slightest risk of a taint on their career. The purpose of such cops was to protect their pension, no matter what the cost.

As a result, when officers like Sharma, Salaskar, Bhosale and Angre stepped up to do the job only a few others were willing to, they also cultivated informants that were different from the rest. These informers were willing to take the risk and provide intel on a target that they knew was slated to be killed. If anyone found out that it was their tip off that led to the encounter, they were sure to die a painful death.

And yet, tip offs kept coming and encounters kept happening. This niche class of informers dug its roots deep into the underworld and kept amassing information even after encounters were stopped. Unfortunately for them, even though they had some really good information on the current activities of the underworld, they found few takers. Not many policemen were willing to go after the gangs the way the police cracked down on them in the earlier days.

Sharma welcomed the informants with open arms. Those that needed money were paid handsomely. Those who needed a favour were helped in every way possible. All this while, Sharma was also in constant touch with his old informants. Everyone knew that Sharma always took care of his own, and everyone wanted their name on that list.

Happy at the sheer feeling of the uniform on his body, Sharma threw himself into his job with the same energy that he had displayed during his first posting at Mahim in 1984.

'I just want to crack one major case,' he said after being reinstated. 'And then I can call it my swansong with satisfaction.'

Sharma created a record of sorts when on Raksha Bandhan day a huge crowd of women thronged his locality. Some 12,000 women tied rakhis on his wrists. Throughout the day, he was seated on a chair below his building and women who had made a huge queue kept piling up a coloured thread on his arm. A sizeable number of burkha-clad Muslim women too had joined the crowd in tying the rakhi on his hand. This spoke volumes about his popularity.

Although he was reinstated on 17 August 2017, it took him a week to get his posting. The same coterie within the force that had orchestrated his arrest in the Lakhan Bhaiya encounter started lobbying against him and ensured that he did not get a posting in Mumbai. All efforts were made to ensure that the words 'tainted' and 'controversial' were attached to his name, while Sharma waited for his fate with a temporary posting to the state control room.

Only one man was willing to take the chance. Then Commissioner of Police, Thane, Param Bir Singh, personally spoke to the DGP and requested that Sharma be posted under him. He agreed to accept full responsibility in case Sharma stirred up any controversies. If there is one officer Sharma holds in high regard in the entire police force, it is Param Bir Singh.

Singh had already chosen a posting for him. After the battle that Sharma had waged against the underworld for years, the senior police inspector of the Anti Extortion Cell (AEC) was the perfect posting for him.

'I'm getting a lot of reports about the underworld threatening businessmen in my jurisdiction, Pradeep,' Singh told Sharma on 24 August, when he was finally attached with the Thane police. 'I need these extortion calls to stop.'

'I'll make them stop, sir,' Sharma promised.

Even Singh was surprised when Sharma started making good on his word less than a month after taking charge.

29

Cop's Chutzhpah

Sharma shifted slightly in his chair as he leaned forward and pressed his left headphone to his ear. The new chair would take some getting used to, he thought.

It had been around two weeks since Sharma was reinstated to the police force as a senior PI and given charge of the AEC of Thane Police. Already, he was aware of the expectations. Everyone was watching to see what his next action would be. His supporters were waiting eagerly; his detractors even more so. News reporters were constantly in and out of his office, the older ones rekindling their rapport with him, the newer ones trying to earn a better place in his memory over the others.

'*Kya sir kab score badha rahe ho*? (When you going to increase your score tally?)' a particularly irritating know-it-all reporter asked, referring to Sharma's string of encounters in his previous stint. Sharma laughed derisively. The days of encounters were passé. It was time to change tactics.

The audio in Sharma's ears was thanks to a call he had received a few days after taking charge. Even as he was floundering to surface from the sheer flood of bouquets, phone calls and well-wishers who flocked to his office at Court Naka in Thane, he received a WhatsApp Call that took precedence over all others. It was a name that had not flashed across his screen for over two years.

'I need to meet you,' the informer said. 'And I can't come to your office.'

Sharma took a second to think. He was simultaneously trying to figure out a place to meet his informant and the level of secrecy required for the meeting, because this was one of his most trusted informants. Something big was afoot.

Finally, he said, '*Mai force mein waapas aate hi ho gaya shuru?* (You started immediately after I joined the force?) How do I know you're not wasting my time?'

'Sir,' the informant said, 'I have been sitting on this for the last two years. Only because I want to give this to you. Trust me, this is important.'

'Okay,' Sharma said. 'Where do you want to meet?'

The informer said that he would wait for Sharma at the Police Officers' guest house not far from his office. Sharma agreed.

'*Mera naam bol* (Drop my name),' Sharma told him. 'I'll see you there.'

Half an hour later, Sharma set out on foot towards the guest house near the Thane Collector's Office, much to the chagrin of his subordinates, who wanted him to take an official car and an armed escort, which was the last thing Sharma wanted. He was perfectly aware of the fact that his enemies were looking out for any chance to strike at him, more so now that he was back in the police, having cocked the granddaddy of all snooks at those who had written him off. But he had made his choice the minute he got off the phone with his informant. Going to meet him with a cavalcade in tow would be like waving a sign proclaiming that the man was his informant. Not to mention it would be professional harakiri.

So, even as his colleagues tried to talk him out of it, Sharma stepped out of the AEC compound, dressed in plain clothes, his personal weapon tucked in his ankle holster, and took the ten-minute walk to the guest house.

The informant was sweating and there was a slight tremble to his hand when Sharma got there.

'I thought you were not coming,' he said.

'Well, I did. What do you have?' Sharma said. His gut feeling told him he was not going to regret coming. But he had to take care not to appear too desperate. It is a control tactic. Informants lose respect for cops who salivate at the slightest mention of a big catch. They need to be conveyed that no matter what they have hidden in their sleeves, the cop is always the one calling the shots.

The informant leaned forward and whispered, despite them being the only men in the room.

'Iqbal Kaskar is running an extortion racket here,' he whispered.

It took a second for the words to properly register with Sharma. He felt a sudden surge of excitement. Iqbal Kaskar was Dawood Ibrahim Kaskar's brother. His nemesis, if the media were to be believed. The fugitive gangster who would fume from his golden throne in Pakistan every time Sharma shot down one of his men. The same Dawood who, after Chhota Rajan split from him, started a rumour that Sharma was killing his men on Rajan's orders.

Unlike his brothers, Iqbal had never relocated to Karachi from Dubai. He continued living in Dubai till his deportation to Mumbai in March 2003. Kaskar who until then had no criminal cases pending against him found a couple of cases slapped against him including one old murder and other extortion cases. Subsequently, he was slapped with the infamous Sara–Sahara case. The case was about building two shopping malls on the land owned by the CPWD. The land was meant for building municipal schools but was encroached by the mafia in collusion with the officials from the Municipal Corporation of Greater Mumbai (MCGM). The investigation which heavily relied on Kaskar and his involvement in the case had fallen flat with the prosecution's failure to indict Iqbal effectively. Kaskar was acquitted and he returned to his den at Pakmodia Street in Dongri, south Mumbai, and begin conducting nefarious activities with impunity.

Iqbal Kaskar had remained untouched by the police machinery since his release from the jail in 2007. However, now his cup of misdeeds seemed to be overflowing with the complaints reaching Sharma's doorstep.

Sharma remained stone faced. But inwardly, he was thinking, this is going to be so much fun.

Over the next two hours, despite Sharma's facade of sustained scepticism, which he worked hard to maintain, his informant told him all the details of Iqbal's little racket.

'It's been going on for years, sir! People here are scared to death. Builders, businessmen, jewellers ... no one is spared,' his informant said.

'*Chal hatt, harami* (Go away, you rascal). Why would Iqbal come from Nagpada to Thane?'

'*Arrey*, sir, he doesn't need to come. What has God given us cell phones? *Udhar Mumbai mein police ne poora tight karke rakha hai* (The Mumbai Police has been quite strict). You don't believe me? Fine. Pick up Mumtaz Sheikh.'

'Mumtaz Sheikh,' Sharma repeated.

'Yes! Motherfucker stays in a flat that they extorted from a builder in Thane. Him and that Israr.'

'Israr who?'

'Israr Sayyed.'

'Give me their numbers.'

Sharma's informant silently dipped into his breast pocket and came up with a slip of papers.

For the next seven to eight days, a team handpicked by Sharma discreetly put together a picture of Mumtaz and Israr's activities. Informants were tapped, past records were sought, call records scanned and cellular locations tracked. Through the call records, as well as independent investigations, the Thane AEC confirmed that Mumtaz and Israr were indeed in touch with Iqbal. It was time for the next step.

'You think C.P. Sir will agree?' PI Rajkumar Kothmire, Sharma's second in command, asked him as they were on their way to meet Thane Police Commissioner Param Bir Singh.

'Only one way to find out,' Sharma said, getting out of the vehicle as it came to a stop at the Commissionerate compound.

Fortunately, Singh agreed with their plan of tapping Iqbal's phone. Singh personally expedited the matter with the higher-ups, and soon Sharma was adjusting the left headphone, which seemed to be slightly defective, as he listened in on Iqbal's conversations.

The hardest part came next. The most crucial aspect for any case of extortion registered by the police is the complainant. While there has been no official study, police officers agree that 90 per cent of extortion cases are never reported to the police simply because the victims are too afraid to speak out. Most, if not all, cases of extortion involve hours and days of cajoling the victim to become the complainant. The terrified victim ends up refusing nine times out of ten.

Sharma spent days meeting the Thane-based builder, assuring him that every possible form of protection would be extended to him. It wasn't easy. After all, this wasn't a Ravi Pujari or a Santosh Pujari. This was Iqbal Kaskar, Dawood Kaskar's brother, whose name featured in every Google search with the keywords 'mafia don'.

The builder was terrified that Iqbal would find out about him registering a complaint and that he would die a slow and painful death in some godown in Madanpura. Sharma gave him his word; not a hair on his head would be touched, and if he cooperated, he would put Iqbal away for a long time.

For Sharma, there was a lot riding on the victim being willing to be the complainant. Firstly, it would help Sharma to put a stop to Iqbal's activities in Thane. Without an official complaint, there was little he, or any police officer, could do on a suo motu basis. But finally, he was ready. He called Kothmire to his cabin and told him to have the team ready the next day.

'Tell no one anything,' he said. 'Instructions will be given at the last minute. Just make sure they are ready to go,' he said.

Sharma was aware of the famous slip given by Iqbal's brother Dawood to the team of officers led by D.S. Soman in 1986 when he raided Musafirkhana and Dawood had flown the coop only minutes before Soman had reached Don's headquarters. There were no cell phones in 1986 yet Dawood got wind of the police team zeroing in on him. Sharma did not want Iqbal to receive intelligence of their crackdown.

'When do we move, sir?' Kothmire asked.

'At night,' Sharma said, smiling. 'When everyone else is winding up.'

Sharma spent the entire night planning every single detail of the operation, going over the plan again and again to make sure nothing had been missed.

He was not just worried about his image if the operation fell through. Granted, he would suffer from loss of face and his detractors would lose no time in telling the world how he fell flat after biting off more than he could chew. They even had WhatsApp at their disposal now to add fuel to the fire, he thought.

But the bigger consequence, if Iqbal managed to escape his clutches, would be that none of his victims would ever file a police complaint again. Sharma was hoping to use this case as a message to other victims, to indicate to them that he would help and that together, they could put Iqbal away for a long, long time. None of that would happen if Iqbal ended up anywhere else other than his lock up.

Around 8 p.m. on 19 September 2017, four civilian vehicles left the AEC compound at short intervals. Each vehicle had one officer who alone knew the real purpose of the expedition. This was revealed to the others after they had turned off their cell phones and deposited them in the glove boxes of their respective vehicles, and even as the dumbstruck cops were digesting the revelation, the loosely formed convoy slid onto Claire Road at Byculla.

Orders were hastily passed given. Each officer was assigned his or her own role. In a busy corner where no one stopped to look at the small group gathered around the tall, burly man, Sharma whispered, 'I know this is short notice. Just use your wits and your experience. You five, identify his lookouts and take care of them. You three deal with the CCTV cameras. Where are the QRT commandoes?'

'Waiting around the corner,' Kothmire whispered back.

'Perfect. Kothmire, you stay in touch with them,' Sharma said. 'You,' he added, pointing at a female officer, 'you are with me.'

One by one, the entire team slipped into the neighbourhood where the Gordon Hall building stands at Nagpada. The building houses the residence of Haseena Parkar alias Hassena Aapa, Dawood's sister who once held court in her house. Iqbal had moved to her place for a while after the 117-year-old Hussaini building, just a couple of buildings away from him, came crashing down in August 2017, killing thirty-four people.

The first few minutes were spent identifying the henchmen that Iqbal had instructed to watch the building's entrance. It wasn't too hard. While they weren't exactly waving signboards with Dawood's face on them, they all had the trademark swagger of a foot soldier working for a prominent gang. One of them was standing by the gate, obviously tasked with running up to his master to alert him at the first sign of trouble. Two of Sharma's officers slowly walked over to where he was standing, not even looking at him till they were directly in front of him. Then, one of them draped a hand over his shoulder and the other lifted the front of his shirt just enough to reveal the butt of his gun before leading him away. The immediate threat had been neutralized.

At the same time, two other officers slid up to the remaining two lookouts and whispered in their ears, telling them to quietly come unless they wanted to be shot down right away. As soon as the last of the lookouts was handcuffed and bundled into one of the cops' vehicles, Sharma and Kothmire began walking to the entrance, the female officer with them.

Silently and quickly, the three cops made their way up to Haseena's flat and Sharma nodded to the policewoman, telling her to go ahead with the plan he had told her just minutes ago. The woman stepped toward the door, while Sharma and Kothmire took their positions on either side, backs to the wall alongside the door, guns drawn. Kothmire's bluetooth earpiece was blinking; he was on a call with his team downstairs, who were waiting anxiously for word from him.

The air was fraught with tension. The female cop rang the doorbell. A shadow fell across the eye hole, as the henchman on the other side regarded her for five to six long seconds. Finally, the shadow moved, and the door was opened.

Following her instructions, the female officer stepped back as soon as she heard the latch being unfastened. By the time the henchman opened the door, he was staring down the barrels of two Glock pistols held by Senior PI Pradeep Sharma and PI Rajkumar Kothmire.

'Get in!' Sharma barked. 'Come on! Get inside! Now!'

'You!' Kothmire said to a second henchman. 'Sit down! And stay that way!'

Without giving the henchman a chance to think, the two cops, shouting orders, forced him inside. Downstairs, the police team heard the two cops through Kothmire's bluetooth earpiece and swung into action. A team of fifteen Quick Response Team commandoes jumped out of their van, which was parked in another lane a few metres away and ran to Gordon Hall. Within seconds, they had formed a cordon around it. Meanwhile, the rest of Sharma's team ran up to Haseena's flat, guns drawn.

Iqbal was completely taken aback. His mouth stayed open and his hand, which held a morsel of chicken biryani from one of his favourite local joints, froze in mid-air as Amitabh Bachchan's famous quiz programme, *Kaun Banega Crorepati*, played on the TV.

Just as the rest of Sharma's team entered the flat, Sharma strode over to the sofa and sat next to Iqbal.

'*Pehchaana*? (Recognize me?)' he asked.

'I ... I read about your comeback in the newspapers...' was all Iqbal could manage.

'Then you know why I am here,' Sharma said.

Iqbal nodded.

'*Khaana kha le* (Eat your food),' Sharma said, picking up the remote and increasing the volume. 'How much has this player won so far?'

Iqbal was picked up along with his henchmen and within days, he was booked under the stringent Maharashtra Control of Organized Crime Act (MCOCA). Sharma was grinning from ear to ear on his first major victory after his return. The media plastered his photograph on the front page and television channels had a field day running the story continuously on their news bulletins.

30

Baba Busts Batla

The Thane Court premises was bustling with activity. Lawyers and civilians milled about the compound as well as its corridors. A young man wiped his wife's tears helplessly as she wept over the fact that bail had been denied to him again. A hardened criminal had a whispered consultation with his lawyer minutes before his case was to come up for hearing. A policeman walked out with a smile on his face, basking in the glow of the fact that his deposition had gone off smoothly, and a conviction was almost guaranteed now.

Amid the hustle and bustle, five officers with the Thane Anti Extortion Cell loitered about aimlessly. But little did the public know that they were keeping a close watch on the entrance.

Just metres away, in a civilian car parked outside a photocopy centre, Senior PI Pradeep Sharma sat in the driver's seat. He had pushed the seat all the way back to accommodate his long legs and had one of his two earphones stuck in his right ear.

The Iqbal Kaskar arrest had brought with it the expected share of pros and cons. On the one hand, Sharma had become an overnight hero. Pictures of him leading Iqbal by the hand out of Haseena's house in Nagpada had gone viral within an hour of the arrest and were still being played out on news channels as the media relentlessly followed the developments in the case. After the builder, from whom Iqbal had extorted four to five flats, two jewellers, too, came forward and registered cases against him. In each case, the Thane AEC got maximum police custody and Iqbal was sure to rot behind bars for a long time. Even after the police custody period expired, the invoking of the stringent Maharashtra Control of Organised Crime Act would ensure that he would not get bail for months together.

On the other hand, however, Sharma's brazen action had ruffled quite a few feathers, in the police department as well as the underworld. Sharma had expected it, but it was a headache nonetheless.

Immediately after arresting Iqbal, Sharma and his team sped to the JJ Marg Police Station, from whose jurisdiction he was picked up, and made a note in the station diary as per protocol. The rules dictate that if a team from a particular Commissionerate conduct an operation in the jurisdiction of another, they have to either inform the concerned police station beforehand or make an entry after the operation. Sharma had never had any intention of informing anyone before the operation because it was too much of a risk. But he had made sure he followed the protocol after the arrest. It would take one wrong move on their part for Iqbal's defence lawyer to get him off on a technicality, and Sharma was taking no chances.

Iqbal's arrest sent shockwaves of rage throughout the Mumbai Police hierarchy. The top brass came down hard on the J.J. Marg police for not knowing what was going on under their noses. Envy took over and attempts to discredit the arrest as a publicity stunt started doing the rounds within a couple of hours. '*Sab nautanki hai* (It's all a big charade),' a former Mumbai Crime Branch officer was telling anyone who would listen. 'When we arrested Iqbal, we just made one phone call to him and he came with his tail between his legs.'

Sharma, who knew he was on firm ground legally, shrugged this off. But it was the other fallout that bothered him the most. Ravi Pujari, a former D-gang henchman, who, for the last couple of decades had not been able to become anything other than a wannabe gangster, called the builder who registered the first complaint against Iqbal.

'*Bahot paisa hai tere paas, madarchod? Muchchad ka financer ban gaya hai tu*? (You have a lot of money, motherfucker? You have become Dawood's financier?)' he asked the builder, referring to Dawood by his derisive nickname. 'Now send me some money or prepare to die.'

The builder ran to the Thane AEC office and almost fainted as he told the officers about the phone call. Sharma, who was in Delhi at the time, giving a report of Iqbal's interrogation, swore left and right when he learned about it and took the next flight to Mumbai. Over the next few days, he picked up several foot soldiers of Pujari's gang.

'What kind of a boss do you idiots have?' he snarled at them. 'We're trying to put a stop to Dawood's activities here, and that *chutiya* [asshole] is trying to mess up our case? Is this the patriotism he keeps boasting about?'

Sharma was referring to a claim that Pujari had often made in his telephonic interviews to news channels about being a patriotic don and a sworn enemy of *deshdrohi*s (traitors) like Dawood, a tactic that was straight out of Chhota Rajan's book.

Nobody believed Rajan's claim in the first place. And coming from Pujari, it was no less than pitiable.

Pujari's foot soldiers conveyed the message to their boss, who finally saw sense and the phone calls stopped.

Everyone around Sharma was talking about how he had made such a big catch within a month of being reinstated. Sharma, however, had already set his sights on other fish in the pond.

When he took charge in August 2017, he drew up a list of criminals who were particularly hated by everyone, policeman and civilian alike. High up on the list was a bookie named Sonu Jalan alias Sonu Malad alias Sonu Batla.

All of five feet tall, Jalan boasted of having connections in high places and was one of the topmost bookies in the country, with links extending to several countries in Asia. Only a few people knew that Jalan had got to the top by blackmailing his way there.

The police had always been wary about Sonu's dirty games. He would call officers with references of other cops and lure them into frank conversations. Unknown to the cops, he would record the conversations and use the one or two stray lines about their financial transactions or their property to blackmail them into submission, threatening to put their superiors or the ACB on their trail.

One such story had recently reached Sharma's ears. Jalan had recorded a conversation with an Assistant Commissioner of Police (ACP) with the Mumbai Police who had led a raid on one of his betting operations. He then started threatening to turn it over to the ACB. The officer, who was nearing retirement, was scared out of his wits at being the subject of an inquiry towards the fag end of his career. The desperate ACP sought a meeting with Jalan and begged him to leave him alone. Jalan is reported to have asked the ACP to spit on the table and then forced him to lick it in exchange for forgiveness.

Sharma could not believe it when he heard it. He first sought out one of the ACP's subordinates, a PI who was now posted with the Thane police and asked him if this had indeed happened. When the PI refused to look up, a furious Sharma made him come to Param Bir Singh and narrate the entire story.

Singh, who was equally enraged, issued a simple order. 'Get him.'

Sharma was aware of Jalan's elusive nature and pulled out all stops. All his informants were tapped. Then, on 17 May 2018, the Thane AEC raided a flat in a residential complex in Dombivli and busted an operation where bets were being accepted on the ongoing Indian Premier League (IPL) series. Everyone who had praised Sharma to the heavens started wondering if he had finally lost his marbles. Why was a celebrated encounter specialist who had just put Dawood's brother behind bars now making Gambling Act cases?

Sharma, however, was not concerned with what they had to say. He had a bigger plan, one which was coming to fruition on 29 May—the day when the remand for the four bookies expired. As they were being taken to court, they were heard bragging that 'Sonu Bhai' would take care of them. In fact, Jalan had managed to convey this message to them through one of his many goons during their last court appearance. Unknown to the smug bookies, this was exactly what Sharma wanted.

As the time drew closer for the bookies to be produced, a car drew up in the Thane Court compound. Jalan, wearing branded clothes and sunglasses, got out with all the panache of a film star.

'Sir, he's here,' one of Sharma's officers said into his earpiece.

'Take him,' Sharma said, quickly getting out of his own car and hurrying to the court.

As Jalan walked towards the court building, the AEC officers surrounded him from all sides. Before he could enter the building, he came face to face with Sharma. The arrogant bookie stared insolently at Sharma's hulking frame.

'Sonu Jalan?' Sharma asked for the sake of formality.

Jalan slowly removed his sunglasses—he thought it made him look cool—and raised an eyebrow. In response, Sharma caught him by his shoulders, spun him around and pushed him into the arms of his officers, who dragged him away in front of his arrested bookies.

'*Aa gaya tumhara Sonu Bhai* (Here comes your boss Sonu),' a constable laughed gleefully as the bookies stared with their mouths open.

Amid curses and promises to teach them all a lesson, Jalan was taken to the AEC office, where he was stripped of his belongings and formally placed under arrest for his alleged links to the IPL betting operation in Dombivli.

Once again, Sharma's phone was ringing off the hook. Senior IPS officers posted in Mumbai called him to confirm if he had indeed arrested the thorn in their side and also to offer their congratulations. They were not just appreciative of his work, they were grateful. Everyone wondered how Sharma had dared to lay a hand on the person that so many cops feared.

Sharma only had one answer: '*Himmat market mein nahi milti* (You can't buy courage in a shop).'

You either have it or you don't.

Sharma made it a point to march Jalan in full view of the news cameras. One such picture—of a subdued Jalan wiping his face with a napkin—was used by the media for weeks on end as the case progressed. Meanwhile, the betting market came to a standstill for a month before it could find its feet again.

As satisfying as it was, Sonu's arrest was only the tip of the iceberg. The car that he had come in belonged to Sameer Buddha, former cop Suhail Buddha's brother. Jalan and Sameer had started a spare parts dealership in 2015, which had failed. The dealership was just one of the many pies that Jalan had had his fingers in.

As Jalan's interrogation progressed, the secrets came tumbling out. The entire nexus that Jalan had built on blackmail was revealed. The most prominent among his victims was the actor Arbaaz Khan. While controversies in the Khan family are usually attributed to Salman, this was the first time Arbaaz found himself in the spotlight for all the wrong reasons.

The police were patient with him. Investigating officers later found out that several appearances that Arbaaz made at public functions were on Jalan's insistence.[10] A stone-faced Arbaaz came to the AEC office for questioning on 2 June 2018.

'I will only say that I am cooperating with the police's investigations,' was all he said to the myriad news microphones shoved in his face before being whisked away by Shera, the Khan family's trusted bodyguard.

If they wanted, the police could have hogged the limelight by slapping charges against all the big names that were uncovered

---

[10] TNN, 'IPL Betting: Arbaaz Khan: Notorious IPL Bookie's Diary Has Dirt on Bollywood, Other Big Names: Cops', Times of India, https://timesofindia.indiatimes.com/city/mumbai/notoriousipl-bookies-diary-has-dirt-on-bollywood-other-big-names-cops/articleshow/64423513.cms.

in the investigation, some of which were never disclosed to the media. However, the purpose was clear from the start: to clip Sonu Jalan's wings; and they stuck to it.

Time and again, Sharma made sure Jalan was brought from the lock up to his office for questioning, knowing fully well that the newshounds were camped in the compound for that one photograph showing Jalan's current miserable condition. The news photographers did the rest, and the once-feared Jalan was now reduced to someone pitiable.

Epilogue

On 4 July 2019, Sharma tendered his resignation to the office of the DGP, Maharashtra, expressing his wish to seek voluntary retirement from the service. The decision, which was taken just a year before he was to finish his service, shocked press reporters, fellow policemen and civilians—everyone except those who are part of his inner circle. Sharma's resignation was officially accepted by the Home Department on 9 September 2019.

An iconic scene from the movie *Zanjeer* (1973) captured the mood of an entire generation. Sher Khan, a powerful hoodlum of Pathan origin, enters a police station. Just as the thug is about to sit on a chair, Inspector Vijay Khanna kicks it away. Sher Khan is shocked by Vijay's temerity. No cop has ever had the gall to behave in this manner. The enraged Pathan glances menacingly at the policeman. 'Better keep standing until you are asked to sit,' says Inspector Vijay Khanna. 'This is not your father's house, but a police station.'

It was a defining moment in the history of Indian cinema, in which a fearless cop is projected with a tough exterior. Amitabh Bachchan as Inspector Vijay Khanna was etched in public memory as the angry young man who was the perennial underdog. He was not only fighting the bad guys but also the system and society. Status quo was unacceptable to this man. True, he was carrying the burden of his past, but he was also determined to change the future. This man did not meekly seek his due from the powers that be. He *demanded* his rights. And the angry young man would stop only when he had attained victory, or salvation, or even martyrdom. Amitabh became an immortal phenomenon and would go on to play several offshoots of the angry young man in *Deewaar* (1975), *Sholay* (1975), *Trishul* (1978), *Kaala Patthar* (1979) and *Shakti* (1982).

As someone who grew up on a staple diet of Amitabh Bachchan's films, Pradeep Sharma incorporated many of the superstar's mannerisms. Some similarities were a mix of coincidence, or fate or perhaps both. Pradeep Sharma also has his roots in the banks of the Ganga. His family hails from Agra in Uttar Pradesh while Amitabh Bachchan hails from Allahabad. Much like the actor, Sharma is also more than six feet tall.

And then, Sharma imbibed mannerisms consciously or unconsciously. When he went to college, he would part his hair like the superstar, his sidelocks would extend down to his ears, and he wore bell-bottoms with full sleeve shirts. Sharma never missed a chance to watch movies in which Amitabh Bachchan played the lead. The fury which seethed within an entire generation on account of widespread unemployment, poverty, inequality and class conflicts was captured perfectly by Amitabh's portrayal of the angry young man. No wonder then, that Sharma imbibed much of the superstar's style and the persona of the characters he played on-screen.

Pradeep Sharma joined the force in 1983 after his training in Nashik. Incidentally, his first posting was in Mumbai, which was his favourite superstar's *karmabhoomi*. But by 1984, Amitabh Bachchan was moving towards a different horizon. The actor took a break from acting and plunged into active politics. He joined long-time family friend Rajiv Gandhi who was heading the Indian National Congress (INC) after his mother's death, and the former Prime Minister of India, Indira Gandhi.

Amitabh was pitted against a heavy weight in the Allahabad constituency. He was fighting against Hemwati Nandan Bahugana, who had served as the Chief Minister of Uttar Pradesh (1973–75), and as State Minister for Communication in the Union Cabinet (1971). As a rank outsider to politics, Bachchan registered one of the biggest victories in Indian history by garnering 68.2 per cent of the total votes polled in the constituency. The margin of the victory left all political pundits dumbfounded. Bachchan was now a Member of Parliament (MP) in the eight Lok Sabha.

Pradeep Sharma had often wondered about the lives of superstars. At the time, there was no bigger actor in the country than Amitabh Bachchan. The man was loved and followed by millions. He had achieved fame and fortune of unimaginable heights. Thousands of fans thronged outside his bungalow in Juhu just to catch a glimpse of their favourite star. What more could a man want? This question had often crossed Pradeep Sharma's mind. And the events of 1984 finally provided him with an answer. Even after everything that Amitabh Bachchan had achieved, he went onto to pursue power of a different kind—political power.

The superstar's achievements before 1984 had delivered only social power to him, and which had provided him with the ability to influence his followers' behaviour and even society.

Political power had perks of its own. As a cop in his early days, Sharma had understood this perfectly. Growing up, Sharma had set his sights on a career in the police force. However, Bachchan's stint with politics made him take notice of the power of the state from a different perspective. That day, Sharma made a mental note of the algorithm of power.

Sharma unwittingly emulated Amitabh in so many ways and yet never acknowledged it. However, he and his wife, Swikriti, were shocked when, one day, their three-year-old daughter, Niketa, pointed towards a magazine cover on which there was Amitabh's picture and said, '*Yeh Daddy hai* (This is Daddy).'

Only those who have monitored Amitabh and Sharma closely will find uncanny similarities in the two men. Apart from physical traits both also have several common episodes in their career. For instance, the only other actor who could boast of such an imposing physique and charm like Amitabh was Vinod Khanna. They both struggled and reached the top together and then Khanna left to join Osho. Amitabh felt unchallenged after Khanna's exit. However, no sooner had Khanna returned than Amitabh quit his booming career in politics and headed to tinsel town once again to reclaim his numero uno position.

Sharma shared similar insecurities with his batchmate Vijay Salaskar. Despite all his achievements, Sharma always felt that Salaskar was the one who could match his laurels. In a batch of encounter specialists, they were regarded as warring superstars.

Khanna eventually succumbed to cancer and Amitabh Bachchan had long since rushed past Khanna in terms of blockbuster hits and popularity. Fate was also tilted towards Sharma as Salaskar was struck down by terrorists in the 26/11 terror attack in Mumbai, leaving him with no competition. Nevertheless, Sharma who once had several encounter specialists to compete with, managed to outlive and upstage all the contenders and survived to remain on top with flying colours, despite his dismissal and arrest.

Sharma is not just a survivor but has insatiable appetite for success. Immediately after news of his resignation—which is still to be formally approved by the DGP's office—became public, people flocked to his office in Thane in hordes, trying to glean some information about his intentions henceforth.

Sharma flatly refused to give any kind of formal statement to the press, saying only that he was waiting for a formal approval before he could speak on the issue.

However, slowly but surely, information started falling through the cracks, as those close to him let it slip that he was intending to contest the upcoming Rajya Sabha elections from Nalasopara on a Shiv Sena ticket.

The choice of the constituency, while surprising for many, was carefully thought out. The constituency is currently ruled by Kshitij Thakur, the son of Hitendra Thakur, who has been a four-time MLA from the region. Nalasopara is a traditional stronghold for the Thakur family and time has brought with it a smug confidence, based on which the Thakurs believe that no one can dethrone them.

What, however, cannot be overlooked, is that this is not Sharma's first foray into politics. While this might be the first time he is actually contesting for a seat, he has, in the past, worked as a kingmaker.

When the then serving chief of Mumbai police, Satya Pal Singh, resigned from his post to contest the parliamentary elections, he called upon Pradeep Sharma to chart his campaign trail for the Baghpat constituency in Uttar Pradesh for the sixteenth Lok Sabha elections. Satya Pal Singh was facing an uphill battle against Ajit Singh, who was then serving as the minister of civil aviation. Ajit Singh hailed from a political family and was the son of the former Prime Minister of India, Chaudhary Charan Singh. How do you defeat someone with such strong political roots? The road to victory would not be easy. But after two decades of service, Sharma had developed a tendency to thrive and deliver under pressure. The Satya Pal Singh success story had whetted Sharma's appetite and he was toying with the idea of joining mainstream politics when he was reinstated as a police officer in 2017.

There are others who say that Sharma's decision to not contest from his own locality in Andheri—where he has lived for a decade and is so famous that even a paanwallah outside the JB Nagar metro station knows his address—is an equally well thought out decision. 'Why earn the enmity from MLAs in your own area when you can break someone else's stronghold and create history in the process?' is how one person in the political circles puts it.

Whatever be the case, Sharma will never forget the lesson he learnt soon at the police academy—'Khaki disciplines the street but it is the khadi that rules the nation.'

That is why, despite having it all, Amitabh quit stardom to make a beeline for Parliament.

Sharma had donned enough khaki and sent someone to Parliament. Now, he was gearing up for his own sublimation to another orbit of power. And time alone will tell that tale.

Acknowledgements

By the year 2003, the feared Mumbai mafia was reeling under the onslaught of 'encounter specialists'. This batch of police officers, who graduated from training in 1983, will always be remembered for the wrong reasons. Their battles against gangsters brought them a huge quantum of fame. Immortality in the annals of the Mumbai Police seemed like the only logical end to their careers.

But way back in 2003, then assistant PI Pradeep Sharma was yet to weather the many impending storms in his life. 'We went against the underworld so hard that I can see our lives getting harder,' Sharma had told me. Some clairvoyance from an officer who is synonymous with the elite encounter squad of the Mumbai Police!

The systemic problem was clear. They had become too big. Guns and bullets had become indispensable in the fight against the underworld. Blue-blooded IPS officers were no longer the toast of the media. So, these 'trigger happy' encounter cops needed to be taught a lesson in humility. A tectonic shift followed in the lobbies of the government and media against these policemen.

In a matter of years, top encounter specialists like Pradeep Sharma, Praful Bhosale, Vijay Salaskar, Ravindra Angre, and Aslam Momin were systematically embroiled in criminal cases, suspended, arrested and dismissed from the force. But in retrospect, the lives and accomplishments of these policemen, including Pradeep Sharma, Praful Bhosale and the late Vijay Salaskar, were quite exciting. Their stories deserved a narration in all flourish and graphic detail. I wanted to pursue such tales much after these men faded into the twilight of retirement. However, a young protégé of mine changed my plans.

Bilal Siddiqi, my sounding board for story ideas, this book would not have been written without your help. But Bilal's intervention hastened the writing of this book. He was instrumental in adding other dimensions to the story which culminated into the digital venture of Red Chillies Entertainment as a feature film on Netflix. For this reason, I dedicate this book to my young and still wet behind the ears pupil, Bilal Siddiqi.

The indefatigable efforts of two of my most promising protégés—Gautam Mengle and Kashif Mashaikh—also made this book possible. Gautam was involved in gathering the research material and the essentials for the story. Kashif was responsible for organizing and structuring the humongous amount of information available on Sharma.

Gautam and Kashif deserve the real accolades for making this story interesting and gripping. Their unflinching devotion helped me complete this book in less than a year in comparison to the others which have taken several years. Thank you, Gautam and Kashif. You are the aces in my pack. Onwards and upwards!

Jigna Vora pitched in with research and interviews for the project. Thank you, Jigna, for completing your assignments before time.

Towards the end of this book, I realized that being an encounter specialist can never be a badge of honour. Not one officer from the Class of 1983 can boast of having loyal colleagues or confidants. In fact, most of their friends and colleagues who chipped in with wonderful anecdotes were wary to be quoted on record. However, I express my gratitude to all officers and their friends for their time and cooperation.

My special thanks to Mr Pradeep Sharma's family, Mrs Swikriti Sharma and her daughters, Niketa and Ankita, who provided valuable insights and perspectives while researching this project.

My publisher, Milee Ashwarya, cannot be thanked enough for believing in me and remaining steadfast till the end of the journey.

My editor, Trisha Bora, was superbly efficient and meticulous.

Finally, this list of thanks will be incomplete without mentioning Mr Shah Rukh Khan, whose faith and encouragement drove me to pick up the gauntlet and finish the book expeditiously.